PACIFIC OCEAN

PHILIPPINES

CERAM

IRIAN JAYA

TERRITORY OF PAPUA AND NEW GUINEA

S I A

AUSTRALIA

A PATTERN OF PEOPLES

ROBIN HANBURY-TENISON

A Pattern of Peoples

A JOURNEY AMONG THE TRIBES
OF INDONESIA'S OUTER ISLANDS

Foreword by Malcolm MacDonald

CHARLES SCRIBNER'S SONS
NEW YORK

Photographs by Robin and Marika Hanbury-Tenison

Library of Congress Catalog Card Number 75-4089
ISBN 0-684-14363-1

Printed in Great Britain

This book is dedicated to Barbara Bentley, Survival International's Director, upon whom Survival International depends; to Shirley Remy, my secretary, upon whom I depend; and, of course, to Marika

I have tried to maintain consistency throughout this book in the spelling of Indonesian words and place names. Bahasa Indonesia, the official language of the Republic of Indonesia, is similar to basic Malay but many European words still originate from the Dutch and the government is fostering the use of purely Indonesian words in the vocabulary. The old spelling of place names is still frequently used and many towns and regions have had their names changed up to four times in the last thirty years, while in some of the remoter areas the correct spelling of local words and the names of tribes have not yet become fully established. Moreover, the outside world is often largely unaware of the new Indonesian names such as, for example, Ujung Pandang for Makassar and Sulawesi for the Celebes. I therefore apologize in advance for the inevitable anomalies which exist.

Contents

Foreword

In this book Robin Hanbury-Tenison presents an informative and pleasing account of the present ways of life of several of the numerous so-called 'primitive' human societies still surviving as minority groups in Indonesia's vast population scattered across its great archipelago of islands. He writes about their often not only characterful but also in some ways admirable cultures—their beautiful arts, crafts and architecture, decorative if scanty costumes suitable for the tropical climate, and traditional moral customs. And he describes how in some cases these are now being seriously eroded—and in all cases threatened—by the intrusion of more modern, sophisticated notions and practices which are either forcibly or persuasively introduced by governmental or other influences. He rightly deplores certain of the ways and speeds at which this is being done. He accepts that, however sad the change may frequently be, it is unavoidable because in our contemporary world none of those peoples can continue to be isolated from other, more 'progressive' communities. The only question is: how, when and to what extent should the modifications in ancient, environmentally suitable manners of living be brought about? Can the tragedy which has overcome, and sometimes completely destroyed, many such societies during the last few centuries as a result of the encroachment of Western and other alien peoples and concepts be avoided? Can what is good (but not what is bad) in their traditional ways of life be preserved and combined with what is good in their true interests (but not what is bad) in more modern cultures?

It is a very difficult, but very important and urgent problem.

I myself have watched a similar dilemma being tackled among the Iban and other tribal peoples in Sarawak, next door to their neighbours in Kalimantan whom the author describes in one section of his book. In spite of the still lingering inclination of the tribal elders when I first knew them in the late 1940's to take heads—a passion which they were no longer allowed to indulge!—those Ibans and the near-by Kayans and Kenyahs were among the most likeable, and in some ways actually whilst in others potentially talented, characters whom I have known anywhere round the Earth. Their skills in certain handicrafts and in music and dancing were delightful; their brains were often excellent; and their ethical code of personal conduct had quite a lot to commend it. They were also then, because of their simple though ample and usually satisfied desires, the happiest people whom I have ever met. I must not expand here on that theme, and will only say that the transition of their younger generation from their customary old, rather jungley ways to more up-to-date, partly urban ones is proceeding not too badly, although considerable difficulties and previously unthinkable frustrations now and then arise.

In my judgement we sophisticated peoples, with our excessive worship of materialist technology, have just about as much to learn from them as they have to learn from us, if our world is to be saved from disaster. I hope that Robin Hanbury-Tenison's writings, as well as similar activities by other individuals and groups dedicated to a great cause, will help to bring us to our senses before it is too late.

Malcolm MacDonald
October, 1974.

Introduction

IN 1973, my wife and I travelled through a large part of the Indonesian archipelago which is not usually visited by outsiders. We spent only a short time in Java and did not go to Bali. Our travels took us through Sumatra, Kalimantan (Indonesian Borneo), Sulawesi (Celebes), Ceram in the Moluccas and Irian Jaya (Indonesian New Guinea). We visited a carefully selected variety of tribal groups representing some of those who, for one reason or another, differ from the national norm and whose cultures and aspirations put them outside the national identity. These people are at the lowest end of the Indonesian social and economic scale; those who have taken the fewest steps on the road to modernity. However, as will be seen, they are not necessarily the poorest or most miserable of Indonesia's citizens. These, the cast-offs of modern society, are more likely to be found living in appalling squalor and hopelessness in jerry-built shanty towns where disease, despair and social unrest fester.

My purpose is not to eulogize the sample of 'isolated' peoples which we saw in Indonesia and assert that all their ways are right and that all progress and development is wrong. Instead, I hope to show that to try to achieve the high ideals set by the Indonesian government for the future, without respect for alternative indigenous values, is a retrogressive step and one that is likely to cause more suffering and misery rather than improvement in the quality of life for all.

I had wanted to go to Indonesia for a long time. In 1957, after leaving university, I travelled through the far east from India to Japan, working on ships and wandering off the beaten track by river boat, country bus and lifts on lorries. But the furthest south I had gone had been Singapore and the then British dependencies in Borneo. Later travels took me to Africa, in particular the Sahara Desert where I lived for a time with the Tuareg and made several long camel journeys in search of prehistoric paintings and rock engravings. However, most of my expeditions over the last fifteen years have been in South America where I gradually became involved in the plight of the Amerindians and their struggle to survive in the face of continuing brutality and oppression. During this time, the pace has quickened as technological innovations and the desire of the governments concerned to open up the interior of Amazonas threatened the Indians' land and accelerated their demise. Eventually, Survival International was formed and we began to try and do something about the problem. This we found could best be achieved by publicizing the situation and drawing the attention of the world to what was happening. But without accurate, up-to-date information on the tribes concerned, and positive recommendations about measures which would assist them to survive, such activities could too easily be dismissed as the rantings of uninformed European pressure groups meddling in the affairs of ex-colonies and developing countries who were now independent and responsible for solving their own problems. I was, therefore, very glad of the opportunity to attempt to demonstrate the constructive uses to which our concern could be put when I was invited by the Brazilian government in 1971 to make a three month tour of many of the Indian areas of Brazil and comment on what was happening and what could be done.

My subsequent report was published by Survival International later that year and my book, *A Question of Survival—for the Indians of Brazil* appeared early in 1973. Although I suppose, inevitably, some elements in the Brazilian régime objected to my very restrained criticisms and assured the world that the recommendations contained in them had all already been seen to, I do believe and hope that they helped to pinpoint the difficulties faced by the Brazilians in dealing with the Indian question. Certainly, the combination of reports by the International Red Cross, whose mission preceded mine, and those of the Aborigines Protection Society and the Minority Rights Group, which followed it, have strengthened the hands of those within Brazil who are trying to implement humane, enlightened policies in this context. Unfortunately, the pressures from those forces obsessed with taming every last hectare of jungle and forcing the indigenous inhabitants to conform to Western ideals of industrial development, are so powerful that, in spite of some successes, the situation throughout South America has continued to deteriorate. It seemed to me that only by widening the focus and making the debate international could any major change of attitude be brought about. If it could be shown that these issues were not unique to South America and that in many other parts of the world similar problems were being faced, with similar successes and failures, then in time perhaps attitudes might change and some progress might be made towards solving what I all too often heard referred to in Brazil as 'the Indian problem'. This was why I decided to visit Indonesia and travel to some of the half a million people there officially classified as 'isolated'.

Throughout, I have tried to assess what we saw in Indonesia from Survival International's point of view. This has not always been easy, partly because the whole picture is such a large and varied one that I constantly found myself having to avoid becoming embroiled in political, social and secessionist questions and partly because so little work had already been done in the direction of asserting the interests and welfare of the tribal groups, that I felt I was often breaking new ground and did not want to begin with false premises. I found early on in my research that to attempt to make direct comparisons between Brazil and Indonesia would be dangerous and misleading. While there are many similarities between the two situations, both superficial and fundamental, there are also deep differences.

Geographically, the scale of the two countries is much the same. The actual land mass of Indonesia, nearly two hundred million hectares (736 512 square miles) is much smaller than Brazil, over seven hundred and fifty million hectares (3 286 470 square miles) but the actual areas covered—nearly five thousand kilometres (3 000 miles) by sixteen hundred kilometres (1 000) miles for Indonesia as against four thousand kilometres square (2 684 miles by 2 689 miles) for Brazil—are more similar. Of course, in Indonesia's case, much of this is sea, but it does mean that transport, whether by air, ship, river boat or truck, must play a large part in the development plans of both nations. The populations, too, fall into the same general brackets. Indonesia, with about one hundred and twenty million people, now has the fifth biggest population in the world, while Brazil, with over one hundred million, lies not far behind. However, more important than this is the distribution in each case, where dense concentrations contrast with vast, sparsely populated areas. Two thirds of Indonesia's peoples live on the islands of Java and Madura, which represent only seven per cent of the country's land surface so that there is considerable pressure to implement 'transmigration' policies on the emptier islands. In Brazil, the bulk of the population is concentrated in a zone stretching only two hundred miles in from the coast, leaving much of the interior almost empty. Here, too, considerable efforts have been made in recent years to encourage people to occupy the remoter parts of the country. With improved communications and exploding populations, this has inevitably meant that the previously isolated and relatively undisturbed indigenous inhabitants of these areas have met an accelerating barrage of outside influences.

The biggest single difference I began to notice between the two cases was that, whereas in Brazil there has been a long history of interest and concern both within and without the country over the dangers which such pressures bring with them to the way of life and, indeed, to the very survival of the tribes affected, in Indonesia the whole question appears to be a new one which is only now beginning to be raised and of which most people seem to be totally unaware. Although in Brazil it can hardly be said that concern with these problems and their wider implications in the field of ecological destruction, conservation of wild life, culture shock and the short-term exploitation of natural resources, has done much yet to influence national policies, at least I nearly always found there that these questions had been raised already and that people were, to some extent at least, aware of them. In Indonesia, due perhaps to the fact that the country has been insulated for a long time from outside world opinion, this was far from being the case. Ideas about the country's development and future were usually expressed in political, military and financial terms rather than scientific and environmental ones.

Another major difference between Brazil and Indonesia, from the point of view of my particular interests in each country is that, whereas in Brazil the Indians are a fairly easily identified section of the community, in Indonesia it is particularly hard to draw the line between truly 'primitive' peoples, and others who are culturally sophisticated but relatively isolated and 'different'. The Indians of Brazil are a numerically small racial minority surrounded, threatened and governed by a vastly more powerful expatriate society originating from Europe, Africa, Japan and elsewhere, who have colonized the country and regard it as their own. Although a very great deal of miscegenation has taken place, both among the colonizing races themselves and between them and the Indians, the remaining indigenous tribes which have retained their identity constitute a section of the community which is quite clearly separate from and outside the national identity. Persistent efforts to change this and integrate the Indians have been the main causes of the problems with which I was concerned there.

The Indonesian problem is not so clearly defined. There are small numbers of jungle nomads on several of the islands whose way of life and general situation bear comparison with some of the isolated Indian tribes of South America; there are the vigorous and numerous peoples of the Indonesian part of New Guinea, who are racially and culturally different from the Indonesians who govern them; and there are many other clearly individual peoples throughout the archipelago who have similar racial origins to, for example, the Javanese, but whose societies and cultures have developed in quite different directions. Moreover, the Indonesian government has always been proudly nationalistic and, since the removal of the Dutch, western-based social science research has been limited and often considered suspect.

For a year before going to Indonesia, I wrote to as many people as possible who had worked there as scientists, missionaries, doctors or civil servants, or whose names I was given as being possibly interested in the same aspects of the country as I was. The response was almost overwhelming and, thanks to it, I was able to plan an itinerary which would give me a general view. But it also made me realize that there was far more to the question of cultural conflict and development in Indonesia than I could hope to cover in one book or, indeed, in one lifetime and that the whole subject was so fascinating and beset by tantalizing red herrings, that I must be careful to explore only those areas in which Survival International might have a legitimate interest.

This meant that I had to look at the basic philosophy which had brought our organization into existence and, in the light of Indonesia's special circumstances, consider what useful rôle we could play. I concluded that Survival International's work has two complementary purposes; humanitarian and practical. In the first place, like most other bodies, we are concerned with a particular section of the world community—in our case tribal peoples—and are disturbed by the suffering, exploitation, degeneration and extinction they so often face when confronted by people who want to change them. We believe that they have a right to the lands that they have occupied, often for thousands of years and often the first members of the human race to do so, and to the ways of life which they have evolved to suit their particular needs. Above all, we believe that they have a right to survive and prosper as equal citizens of whatever nation has grown up around them.

Secondly, it is becoming apparent that they may have a practical rôle to play in the world today as conditions and values change. It is surely no longer open to doubt that all is not well with our planet and with mankind. Viewed from satellites and from the moon, the earth is seen to be small and fragile. Diminishing resources combined with an exploding population and increased material aspirations have caused a widening of the gap between the 'haves' and the 'have-nots' and necessitated major reassessments of the direction in which we are heading. Doubts have been expressed about the viability of continuing to expand productivity and economic growth indefinitely and it is suggested that we may be losing more than we gain in the process. The promises of the Industrial Revolution are not being fulfilled and it appears that, for the vast majority of people, the quality of life is not improving. The horrors of global wars, famines and epidemics are as near, or nearer, than ever. Perhaps we have developed too quickly over the last few centuries and the cause of our confusion and fear today lies in the strangeness of the selves we know. Perhaps the shock to our own society is more than we can take and this in itself accounts for some of the problems we face. We may overcome these difficulties through our own abilities and resourcefulness. Miraculous technological innovations may provide the bases for new support systems. But a logical, sensible and vitally important step in the search for where we went wrong and what we can do about it is to listen to and learn from those societies which have not yet fallen into the same chain of errors.

To hope that such attitudes may come to play a part in Indonesian thinking is not entirely fanciful. Although the country is dominated by the Javanese and administered on the whole by the military, the people throughout the spread of islands making up the nation belong, with the outstanding exception of the Papuans of Irian, broadly speaking to one race. Although there are innumerable regional, provincial, tribal and local rivalries dividing the different peoples, there is no major ethnic division sufficient to create a colonial situation within the country (again with the exception of Irian). The people work together whatever region they come from and, although their local customs and traditions may be different, there is no desire to impose these on others. They are recognized as equally valid to those of a man's own region and certainly worth respecting. Only two philosophies are generally found being promoted energetically throughout Indonesia. One is Islam and the other is what I shall call for want of a better description, 'western modernity'.

In several areas Islam is followed with varying degrees of fanaticism—Christian churches are occasionally damaged or burnt down and Europeans (assumed to be Christian) are viewed with suspicion. These regions have also contributed largely to the political unrest during the years since independence and have been the main centres of secessionist movements.

On the whole, however, the Indonesians, and in particular the Javanese, although nominally Muslim, are both lax in their religious observance and very involved in the traditions and superstitions, beliefs, customs and cultures dating from long before the arrival of Islam. The word for these is *adat*, perhaps the most significant single feature of Indonesian life and one which influences, in one way or another, almost everyone in the country from the highest government official to the humblest peasant. Wise men, astrologers, oracles and mystics are consulted on important issues by generals and businessmen and I was told that even the President and his Cabinet have, on occasion, devoted considerable time to matters concerning *adat*. For example, after the coup of 1965 and while Sukarno was still alive but living under house arrest, the new régime were very worried because it was widely thought that he had in his life received the ninth *kris*. This is an Indonesian dagger with a scalloped cutting edge and serpentine blade, often beautifully decorated and believed to have a spirit of its own. A *kris* should not be bought, but must be given to you or inherited and legend has it that if you have received nine of them you are invincible. Cabinet meetings were held to discuss this problem and it was eventually decided that the only power strong enough to combat Sukarno would be to possess the *Gaja Mada*, a famous Balinese mask which had belonged to Bali's greatest hero. It was arranged that this mask should be lent to Suharto for a time and it is widely believed that this is how he was able to overcome the residual threat represented by Sukarno until his death in 1970.

President Sukarno's greatest achievement was to unify Indonesia. He made one nation out of a widespread and diverse group of islands and peoples, kingdoms and races, previously administered through historical accident and the treaties of colonial powers by the Dutch. For the first few years following independence in 1945, there were many attempts by parts of the new nation to secede and the country was beset by acute economic and political problems as it struggled to achieve a national status and identity. These culminated in the attempted communist coup of 1965 which led to the decline of Sukarno's authority and the vesting of most legislative and executive power in the military.

Now the country is relatively stable and preparing for an economic boom. Its wealth in minerals, timber and agricultural resources is enormous, but the population is growing fast and the government faces huge problems in its efforts to improve the people's standard of living. These are not made any easier by the corruption and nepotism built into the system which tends to concentrate wealth and power in the hands of a few and leaves the majority progressively poorer. A familiar pattern in many developing countries is emerging and if Indonesia is to avoid the upheavals which so often accompany such rapid changes, it is necessary to consider the nation's special characteristics and the options open to it.

Indonesia is unquestionably rich and although perhaps not as fabulously wealthy as is sometimes made out, it is likely, if only through its sheer size and strategic situation, to become one of the world's leading powers. But, at the moment, through lack of working capital, sufficient trained technocrats and adequate infrastructure, most of its riches are exploited by foreign companies using expatriate labour and remitting the proceeds abroad. There is some of the richest land in the world in Indonesia and some of the finest farmers, yet rice, the predominant food, is imported. There are signs that the Indonesians themselves are beginning to resent this state of affairs and to demand that more attention is paid to eliminating poverty and making the country self-sufficient than to improving the balance of payments by allowing their natural resources to be extracted by foreigners.

As this book goes to press, reports are coming from Indonesia of rioting by students in Jakarta against 'Japanese economic exploitation' (*The Times*, January 17th 1974). An all-night curfew was imposed on the city and schools and universities were closed during a visit by Mr Tanaka, the Prime Minister of Japan.

Other reports indicated that the demonstrations were not so much specifically anti-Japanese as an opportunity to express widely felt grievances over the corruption of government officials and the ostentatious life-style of the rich generals. While the nation's new found wealth from oil, minerals and timber is exploited by foreign interests and the Indonesian balance of payments situation improves dramatically, the per capita income of the people remains at ninety-five dollars (*Time*, January 28th 1974), one of the lowest in the world.

The cultural diversity of Indonesia is unique. No other country has so rich a spectrum of customs and peoples, each with its own special skills and knowledge of the particular environment in which it lives. The Bugis of southern Sulawesi were sailing and trading between Australia and Madagascar before the Portuguese rounded the Cape of Good Hope. Inshore fishermen visit each of Indonesia's 13 677 islands (by one count) as well as innumerable reefs, lagoons and rivers. Inland, over three hundred ethnic groups, speaking more than two hundred and fifty distinct languages and uncounted dialects, farm and hunt from the snow-capped mountains of Irian to the jungle swamps of Sumatra. Each has adapted, often over thousands of years, to its own particular circumstances and needs. Out of these has grown a colourful and fascinating variety of customs and traditions with their arts and crafts, abilities and techniques. Now, with the sudden influx of western products and ideas, these are all too often being degraded and forgotten as cheap, plastic goods flood in from Singapore and Hong Kong and development projects, which produce quick and short-term results and often leave a wilderness behind, supplant tried and tested systems.

PART ONE

❧

Sumatra

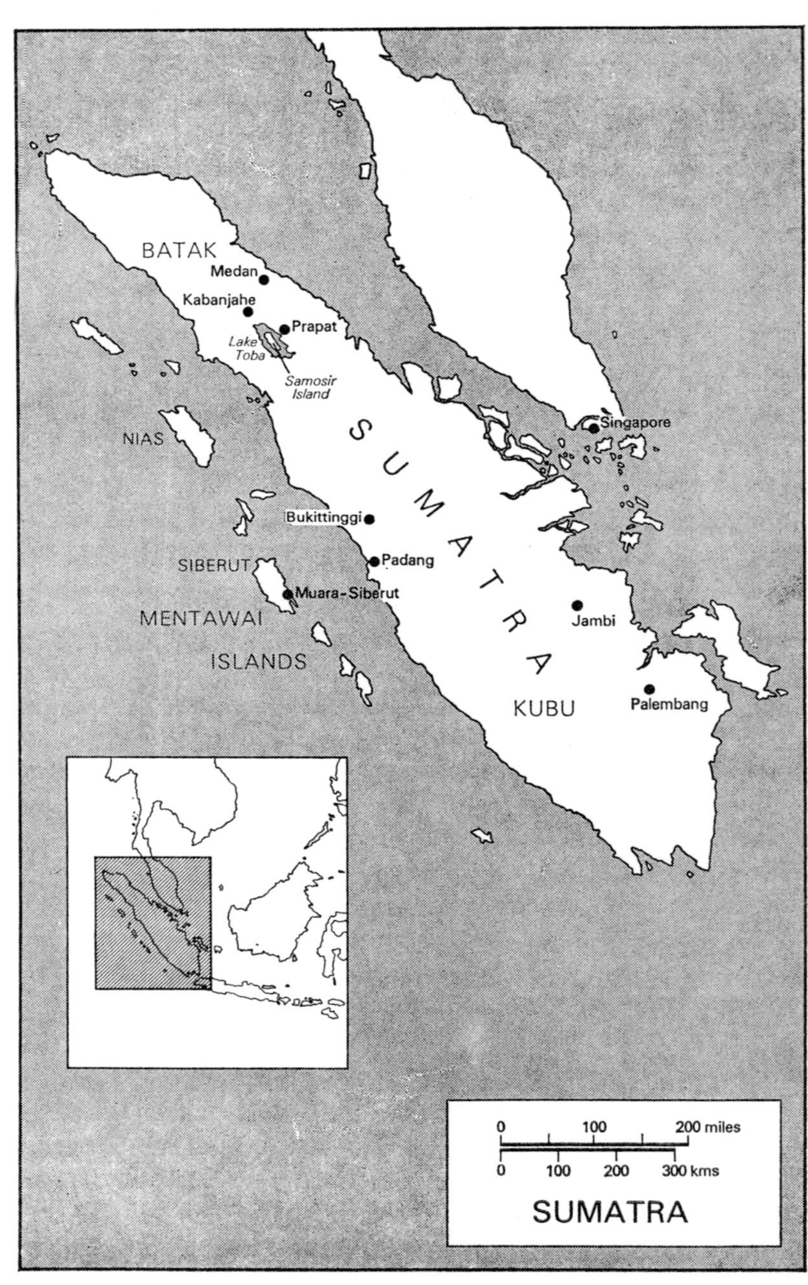
BATAK
Medan
Kabanjahe
Prapat
Lake Toba
Samosir Island
NIAS
SUMATRA
Singapore
Bukittinggi
Padang
SIBERUT
Muara-Siberut
MENTAWAI
ISLANDS
Jambi
KUBU
Palembang
0
100
200 miles
0
100
200
300 kms
SUMATRA

The Bataks

On the 3rd March 1973, we left England and flew to Jakarta. There I wanted to see and talk to some of the people who had kindly supplied so much advice on where to go in Indonesia in order to gain as wide an impression in the time available. The danger with this was that everyone had different ideas and if I had spent long in such talks we would have ended up with a programme requiring three years rather than three months.

I also had to arrange the necessary permits to stay for the full three months and go to all the places we might, if we were lucky, have time to visit. It soon became clear that, if I were to approach these problems from the point of view of a piece of scientific research, the bureaucratic formalities would be endless and we would never get anywhere. In any case, I did not see our purpose as such. Neither of us represented official bodies, nor had we been to Indonesia before. Even Survival International was not financially involved, the journey being privately financed with the help of advances from our respective publishers and a grant from one foundation with no strings attached. We were not pretending to conduct in-depth research, but merely to have a first general look at the country with particular reference to certain areas and aspects which interested us. We were therefore tourists and, as such, life suddenly became much easier. With the exception of Buru, the island on which some ten thousand political prisoners are interned, we could go anywhere and see anything we wished. An extremely efficient Jakarta travel agency, who impressed me at the outset by rescuing a drawerful of clothes and film which had been left behind in a hotel during our stop-over in Singapore, arranged for the extension of our visas and made the bookings on all the internal flights between the various centres, serviced by the state airlines *Garuda*, meaning 'eagle', and *Merpati*, meaning 'dove'. From there on, we would be on our own, but even then I was hopeful that we would succeed in reaching some of the tribes I had been advised to visit, since I had received encouraging letters from, or been given the addresses of, at least one or two people who would help us on each island.

Only in Jakarta itself did the whole project seem impossible. Most of those we met had not been further from Java than Bali and regarded the outer islands as remote, dangerous and uncomfortable places from which we would be unlikely to return. We were warned repeatedly that travel into the interior would be slow and difficult with delays in terms of months rather than days and every possible hazard, such as shipwreck and robbery, awaiting us at every turn. In fact, the problems were largely exaggerated but, as it turned out, we were extraordinarily lucky to complete our altogether over-ambitious plan in such a short time. That we did so was entirely due to the generous help and advice we received everywhere, from Indonesians and expatriates alike.

After only two days in Jakarta, we realized that, as is so often the case, the longer we stayed, the more we would find to delay us. We would have to return at least twice more since there were no direct flights between Sumatra and Borneo and on to Makassar. This meant that we could travel light, leaving most of our things in a friend's house in Jakarta and, as I had expected to spend a week there, gain a few days on what now seemed our hopelessly optimistic schedule. We planned to begin by visiting three contrasting groups in Sumatra and then work our way east to end up in New Guinea. We flew first to Medan in northern Sumatra and then travelled inland, by collective taxi, to Lake Toba where we crossed to the island of Samosir, the very heart of Batakland.

* * *

THE BATAKS

The Bataks are one of the most successful as well as one of the largest cultural minorities in Indonesia. For centuries they were feared as powerful magicians and cannibals, regarding all strangers as enemies. It has been suggested that Herodotus was referring to them when he spoke of *Padaioi* or cannibals. Certainly, they first became celebrated in the late eighteenth century when Europeans were amazed to hear of a cultured and literate people who nevertheless practised anthropophagy. In fact, they ate only captives and criminals but the way they are reputed to have gone about it should satisfy the most bloodthirsty reader. Edwin Loeb, in *Sumatra, its History and People,* published in 1935, quotes an eye-witness as follows:

> The captive is now bound to a stake in an upright position. A number of fires are lighted in the vicinity, the musical instruments are struck and all of the customary ceremonials are observed. Then the chief of the village in which the ceremony takes place draws his knife, steps forward and addresses the people. For among the Bataks nothing is done, no matter of how evident a nature, unless all the reasons for the contemplated action are discussed beforehand. It is explained that the victim is an utter scoundrel, and in fact, not a human being at all, but a *begu* (ghost) in human form, and that the time has come for him to atone for his misdeeds. At this address, the people water at the mouth and feel an irresistible impulse to have a piece of the criminal in their stomachs, as they will then rest assured that he will do them no further harm. This is the expression they themselves use to explain their cannibalism. According to their description, the pleasure which they feel in satisfying their revenge in this manner, and the consoling quiet which it gives them, is not to be compared to anything else. All draw their knives. The *radja* cuts off the first piece, which varies according to his taste, being either a slice of the forearm or a cheek, if this be fat enough. He holds up the flesh

and drinks with gusto some of the blood streaming from it. Then he hastens to the fire to roast the meat a bit before devouring it.

Now all the remaining men fall upon the bloody sacrifice, tear the flesh from the bones and roast and eat it. Some eat the meat raw, or half raw, in order to show off their bravery. The cries of the victim do not spoil their appetite. It is usually eight or ten minutes before the wounded man becomes unconscious, and a quarter of an hour before he dies. The remainder of the flesh then is cut from the bones (and eaten that same day) and the skeleton buried outside the village.

In the nineteenth century, Rhenish-Lutheran missionaries started working with the Bataks, concentrating on schools and education. One wonders how many of them were eaten in the process, but their efforts were successful and today over a third of the one and a half million Bataks are Christian, the remainder being equally divided between Muslim and pagan. They are a hard-working and capable people, with their own written language, strong cultural traditions and great ability as craftsmen. They build large, beautifully decorated houses on piles and are energetic farmers and traders. They were among the earliest peoples in Indonesia to adopt wet rice systems which may have been introduced from India as early as the sixteenth century. This is one of the reasons for their relative prosperity and the density of their population.

Wet rice cultivation, known as *sawah* depends on the availability of water which is required to aerate the soil and deposit nutrients on the paddy fields. This in turn involves considerable management skill and cooperation so that each field can gradually be flooded as the crop grows and then be drained off after the rice flowers so that the field is dry by harvest. The great advantage of the *sawah* system is that a stable yield can be produced year after year without any fallow periods. With intensification and improved techniques, output can be increased to a remarkable degree to support a growing population. The extreme examples of this have been in Java where, in certain areas, a staggering two thousand two hundred people per square mile live virtually by agriculture alone and nearly half the districts on the island have *rural* densities of over thirteen hundred per square mile. To put this in perspective and realize how dense a population per square mile this really is, one should bear in mind that the overall average density of the whole world, including cities and towns, is seventy, Europe, the most densely populated continent has two hundred and forty-six people per square mile and Holland, Europe's most crowded country has under one thousand, again including cities.

However, *sawah* production at these high levels of production is only possible when the soil both of the fields themselves and over which the irrigation water runs contains sufficient nutrients. In the cases of Java and certain areas of Sumatra, including Batakland, these are largely provided by the fallout from the many active volcanoes. Elsewhere, shifting cultivation, or *ladang*, is more usually practised. This is the oldest form of agriculture and has been practised throughout the world since prehistoric times. Now it is mostly confined to the tropics where, although it is usually associated with low population densities, its importance and potential, particularly in relatively infertile and ecologically delicate areas, are being increasingly studied. In the past, the general assumption that *sawah* was superior to *ladang* has led to the neglect of sufficient study of the rôle shifting cultivations can play in food production. Today it is recognized that *ladang* is often the more rational use of land, particularly in densely forested areas with weak soils.

Many Bataks have become teachers and doctors and risen to high rank in the Indonesian government. Yet they are proud of their traditions and of their identity. When possible, they prefer to be returned to their homeland to be buried in ancestral graves. Large numbers still live according to the old ways and are not despised for doing so. Even cannibalism still crops up now and then. We heard of a case that had taken place only a few months before our arrival, when a Batak boy had been executed and some other young men gaoled for the ritual killing and eating of a girl from another group with whom the boy had fallen in love. Apparently, they had done this at the instigation of the boy's father, who had said it was the only way to appease the spirits.

I felt that it would be interesting to visit the Bataks first as a successful group and see if I could learn from them any lessons which could be usefully applied to some of the more fragile and threatened peoples we were to meet later. Besides, they inhabit a high, mountainous region of great beauty and we looked forward to a brief change from the equatorial, sea-level steam into which we had plunged, straight from an English winter.

Lake Toba was certainly beautiful. It is by far the largest lake in Sumatra, being ninety kilometres (fifty-six miles) long and thirty kilometres (nineteen miles) wide, very deep and blue and lying at nearly twelve hundred metres (four thousand feet), with cliffs and hills and irrigated rice fields around the edge. We had an introduction to a young Batak who lived on the island of Samosir on the lake, the spiritual centre of the Toba Batak people. His name was Mangoloi and we hoped to stay with him as there is no accommodation on the island, most of the inhabitants still practising the traditional way of life surrounded by the tombs of their ancestors. The dramatic scenery of the lake has attracted tourists for some time and we found that Samosir has recently become a staging post for hippies on the Bali trail. Inevitably this was bringing some problems as bikinis, pot and free love were encountered by the rather prudish Bataks for the first time. Mangoloi's hospitality was being enjoyed by no less than twenty-six young people of various nationalities and although he was coping well with the situation, providing bed and board at a minimal ten pence per night, he confirmed that he was worried about the future.

He had already had some trouble from the police who objected to such goings on and from residents and, in particular, hotel owners from the town of Prapat opposite on the mainland who saw potential customers passing them by. Lake Toba is being developed as a tourist resort, but travel there is still fairly uncomfortable and slow so that not many arrive although we heard of plans to bring passengers up by bus from cruise ships moored in Medan. Mangoloi's own ideas were sound and should, I felt, be encouraged. He does not think that the island of Samosir itself is a suitable place for hotels as they would spoil its unique character. He is interested in protecting the remaining old houses and looking after the tombs and sacred places which his own people like to visit themselves.

Since tourists will come anyway, it is pointless to pretend that they will not bring change with them and influence the Batak way of life. Instead, they should be given what they want while, at the same time, ensuring that the Batak people benefit in the exchange. Most new Batak houses, even if they are built in the old style are roofed today with corrugated iron since this is cheaper and involves less labour to build. If the tourists want to see houses with roofs made of palm fibre then they must pay. For the government to subsidize the construction and maintenance of traditional houses in Sumatra is no different in principle from the Arts Council giving grants to thatch cottages in Devon. At Prapat on the shore of Lake Toba, active encouragement is being given to the hotel and tourist industry. The visitors spend money on accommodation, meals and shopping in the town as well as boats and tours of the lake. They want to enjoy the superb scenery enhanced by the delightful Batak villages on the island and to have the chance of seeing a picturesque and perhaps enviable traditional way of life being practised. If the Toba Batak people want to cash in on this, and it seems they have little choice in the matter, then it is only sensible to provide what is required.

I find the whole question of tourism and its usually corrosive effect on the regions and people subjected to its influence one of the most difficult issues to resolve. But it is a force that cannot be ignored and the earlier decisions are taken as to how it can best be contained and exploited, the less undesirable side effects are likely to follow.

Mangoloi wants to encourage the building and restoration of original Batak houses. Before outboard motors came to the lake, large dugout canoes with sails used to ply across the water and he knows of one or two of these now lying disused. Restored and used commercially or as pleasure boats on the lake, they would add a whole new dimension to the view and the opportunity of drifting past a complete scene from pre-contact Batakland would surely be a most desirable tourist attraction.

But then again, the whole idea of encouraging people to wear a traditional and perhaps uncomfortable costume when sweat shirts and jeans and gumboots are available in the local market, is somehow paternalistic and rather nauseous. Persuading them to use old-fashioned tools which involve more hard work than manufactured labour-saving devices, condemning them to hours of back-breaking toil in the rice fields, when the job could be done by a tractor with modern equipment, is not only cruel and oppressive but does not even make economic sense.

However, a subsistence economy, providing few opportunities to save, does not pay for modern clothes and tractors. If labour-saving machinery is introduced, a proportion of the labour force will become redundant and need other forms of employment which is unlikely to be directed to remote inland areas when there is such overcrowding and such a surplus of manpower in the urban concentrations around the coast. If the young people do leave to work in the cities the region which, under the old system supported a large and relatively prosperous community, may stagnate and become in the long run less productive. The tourists, with their modern gadgets and obvious wealth, arrive creating needs and desires for unfamiliar objects from radios to razor blades but they want to see people acting as they did in the past.

The dilemma is compounded and it takes a wise man to see what is valuable in his own culture and to appreciate the usefulness of new and marvellous things without becoming blinded to the faults of either, or dazzled by their virtues.

This is a problem common to all peoples at all stages of industrialization and development and it is one to which there are no easy answers. Each case is different and everybody must decide for themselves what to keep and what to reject. Keep too much from the past and your cultural attic is cluttered and stifling. Throw away everything and you are in a cultural void.

Many Bataks have made the transition successfully and with confidence to become leading citizens in the larger and different context of Indonesian society. What are the reasons for their success when so many other societies have vanished, vegetated or been vanquished? Perhaps they are genetically superior people with an innate ability to work harder but there must be other factors involved and one of these is probably their strong sense of identity, both as a people and with their homeland. This has provided a secure cultural base from which to grow. If this is true, however, it does mean that when the spiritual centre is threatened by processes which may mean that its character and identity are changed beyond recognition, it would be as well for the Bataks to take notice.

I admired Mangoloi for concerning himself with these problems and trying to do something about them. He had been brought up by an uncle who worked for the World Bank in Medan on the coast and was educated there before going into the civil service. But he had decided early on to return to Samosir where his father, one of the hereditary chiefs of the island, owned a stretch of rather barren hillside and lakeshore. He spoke good English and controlled his horde of assorted visitors with great presence and aplomb, which can't have been easy. On the whole they did as they were told.

He took us on his boat to visit his father at the far end of the island. Four other young Bataks came with us and it was interesting to see how well they respected Mangoloi, not just as an obvious leader but also very much as one of them who just happened to be stronger and better at everything than they were. A lot of the time they sang in excellent close harmony songs which reminded me of German beer gardens and the Swiss Alps; very melodic with catchy tunes and much yodelling. Perhaps high mountains and clear, cool air affect the sort of music which develops.

The shore of the island is almost unbelievably romantic. Grassy banks with little bright, white sandy beaches, lie along the water's edge. Every inch of flat land behind is covered with vivid emerald green rice paddies, terraced wherever there is a gentle hillside and networked with tiny canals and water-courses, simple bamboo sluices and diminutive splashing waterfalls. Black water buffaloes tread delicately along the terraces, eating only the grass on the edges, never the rice, and watched over by small children.

Above and on the steeper slopes, the bare mountainsides soar up to the high central plateau of the island, but in the uncultivated valleys and gorges the jungle is as lush and varied as a botanical garden. The houses are nearly always hidden in dense clumps of trees and there is usually a group of five or six in a straight row, sometimes with rice stores opposite. The roofs are boat-shaped, rising to high pointed ends at the eaves and although not quite as romantic as the Toraja houses we were to see later in Sulawesi, they are a remarkable sight. When reroofed with corrugated iron and painted with red ochre, the original design was always faithfully preserved and the result not unattractive but those still covered in palm fibre looked immensely powerful and solid. As Mangoloi said, proudly pointing out one which he claimed was over a century old, 'Would a tin roof last that long?'

Inside it is dark and warm with a dry floor made of bamboo slats through which the massive round supports emerge from the ground six feet below. These pass through the ceiling into the upper chamber and below the point at which they disappear into the roof a large circular wooden disc four feet across and six inches thick prevents rats from coming down into the room. In the centre is an open cooking fire, the smoke from which blackens the rafters and then goes on up to pickle and preserve the thatch. The outside of the house under the eaves is carved and painted with a great variety of designs and patterns and in the front there is a small balcony reached through a low door.

Everywhere we went, we were warmly welcomed and offered fruit or a drink. The children were very friendly and cheerful and the Bataks' natural hospitality was made almost embarrassing by the presence of Mangoloi who was obviously extremely popular. Part of the reason for our boat journey was to collect the remaining carved timbers from some old houses which had fallen down and which Mangoloi intended to rebuild at a new site. Beer and rice wine were pressed on us as we loaded the heavy poles on board and at each settlement we were encouraged to stay longer so that our progress along the shore was slow.

It was well after dark by the time we returned to Tomok, Mangoloi's village, and the hippies were waiting to be fed. He arranged everybody in a circle on the floor of his house, placed bowls of food—rice, fish, spiced meats, plantains and vegetables—in the centre and then, on the command 'Go', we all reached in and filled our plates.

Scattered all over the island are stone tombs shaped like small Batak houses and these are whitewashed and protected by the inhabitants. High on the hillside with green fields below and a fine view out over the water to the hazy mountains beyond I could see, as we sat on one of the stone graves, how any Batak would wish to return here to be buried.

The island is also quite fertile and vegetables are traded with the mainland. We walked a few miles to a village called Amarita where we spent a night before leaving at dawn on a boat, taking produce to the market at the far north of the lake. Sacks of onions, potatoes, shallots and carrots, live pigs with their feet trussed together and baskets of all shapes and sizes were piled on the deck for the long run across open water to the distant shore. The lake was as smooth as glass without a breath of wind. Everyone was laughing and a little overexcited by the prospect of the market, particularly when another boat appeared round a headland and began to pull alongside. Like in the great grain races, it really mattered who reached the buyers on the shore first and we encouraged our tired old diesel engine with songs and shouts echoed from our rival until both boats arrived together at the usual market bedlam on the beach in front of the town.

Kabanjahe, an hour's drive north of the lake, is the centre of the Karo Bataks. There we stayed with a young anthropologist who took me on the back of his motorcycle to a village some distance from the town. The Karo Batak houses are much bigger than the Toba Bataks'. Each one contains eight families, with four family fires. The ends of the houses are beautifully carved and at the eaves' ends and also sometimes on an extra tower stuck on top, there are dried buffalo heads with the horns still on. The men, on the whole, wear European clothes, and the women sarongs with little shirts on top. They have horses and water buffalo and grow cabbages and other vegetables which they used to export to Malaysia. During confrontation, this trade was stopped and now the Malaysian and Singapore people have developed other sources so that the economy of the Karo Batak is very depressed. Once again, it is superbly beautiful country, with high valleys of rice fields, some irrigated wet rice *sawah*, and also large areas of dry rice, *ladang*, which does not require constant flooding.

We sat and talked in one of the houses with an old lady

who gave me betel to chew. This is not a particularly attractive practice, although I suppose no worse than smoking, involving as it does a lot of spitting of the resulting red liquid which also stains the mouth and teeth. I found the taste quite pleasant. Through the open door of the large communal house, we could see a range of high hills on the horizon. 'There are many traditional villages there', the anthropologist had told me, 'but they can only be reached on foot. It is quite probable that no European has ever been there except perhaps an occasional Dutchman in the very distant past. There, one would receive complete hospitality like in the old days, but without the risk of being eaten anymore. All Bataks, even those who are still pagan, know the law now and a visitor would always be safe. But their pattern of life is changing and this is causing problems. The men used to fight each other a lot and this kept them busy while the women worked in the fields. Now that they are no longer allowed to fight, young men tend to hang about on street corners since the idea of work is alien to them.'

He obviously had a good relationship with the Bataks and they liked him and listened to him. As an anthropologist, he said he had been trained to view change over a timescale of fifty or hundred year periods and to accept it as inevitable and indeed desirable as part of a society's development. We were in complete agreement that when change comes too fast, that is in five or ten years, then culture shock is caused—even to sophisticated peoples like the Bataks. I told him that I believed part of Survival's job was to involve scientists in the realities and implications of what they were studying. All too often, work which brought a close understanding and intimacy with a tribe or society resulted in a purely academic assessment of their problems rather than practical efforts to solve them or suggestions about how to insulate people against the ill-effects of rapid change.

We also agreed that solutions usually involved the question of a peoples' identity but that this was a particularly tricky subject to discuss in Indonesia because of the strong separatist movements and the government's difficulties and preoccupation with unifying the country. As a result, such talks could be regarded as a threat to national security and with more justification than, for example, in Brazil where the tiny Indian minorities never did and never could threaten war or secession, although they have regularly been accused of both.

Perhaps Indonesia would be better run as a federation rather than by a central government based physically and psychologically in Java. If this were ever to come about, power would be transferred to the regions but this would not affect the Bataks greatly one way or the other. They have never been a unified people, or grown together into a single state, so that their sense of identity would not necessarily be strengthened by any such move. Although modern man tends to reduce most issues to political or economic terms, these are not necessarily relevant to the problems of cultural minorities. Since I first became interested in Indonesia, I had felt that the individuality and identity of the minorities scattered throughout the islands was the key to their problems and perhaps to their survival. If that were the case with a big and successful group like the Bataks, how much more would it be true of the smaller and weaker peoples we were to see later.

Siberut

❧

FLYING down the Sumatran coast to Padang, we stared out to sea hoping for a glimpse of the island of Siberut some seventy miles away to the west and worrying about the fierce rainstorms we could see lashing the water below. We flew over tiny round islands and sunken reefs—and very few boats. We speculated on what we would do if our contact let us down, how we would set about reaching Siberut and what we ought to take in the way of equipment.

All these problems were resolved the moment we landed. We were swept away by a sturdy, blond German, who grabbed all our baggage and disappeared into the crowd with it to 'fix everything'. This was Helmut Buchholz and, on the basis of one short letter from me, posted hopefully in Cornwall some weeks before and a garbled telephone call I had made to his wife from Jakarta, in which I certainly hadn't been able to hear a word she was saying but had hoped she could hear me, he had made all the necessary arrangements for us to go to Siberut.

To cross to the island and spend a week there, he had had to hire a twenty-ton tramp steamer with its Chinese skipper and crew of four and pay them to sit in the bay until we were ready to return. Ships go there so irregularly that, had he not done this, we might have been stuck there for a couple of months. Moreover, because he had saved the skipper's life during the troubles in 1965, it was costing only ten pounds a day although no other boats were available and there was no other way of getting there, since there is no airstrip.

Siberut is the largest of the Mentawai islands and it has only rarely been visited by outsiders. Even the Dutch did not allow their personnel to go there until 1925 due to the unpredictability and supposed savagery of the inhabitants. It is about eighty miles long by thirty miles wide with a population of some sixteen thousand islanders, the descendants of a proto-Malay people who may have been the earliest men to inhabit any part of the Indonesian archipelago. There are also a few Catholic and Protestant missionaries as well as some police and traders from the mainland. Of all the peoples we met in our travels through Indonesia, the Mentawaians reminded us most of the Indians of South America. They are also facing many similar problems. Rival missionary groups vie for their souls; fanatical Muslim police have in the past forbidden them from keeping pigs, wearing decorations, tattooing their bodies, growing their hair long and living in communal houses; large foreign lumber companies have leased concessions over most of the island, moving in heavy crawler tractors to extract the trees and bringing with them alien diseases. Efforts have been made to resettle the Mentawaians in 'model' villages on the coast where their clan life is disrupted and boredom and degeneration set in.

Low ranges of hills, swamps, rivers and dense forest cover the land which has an excessively high rainfall of over three thousand millimetres (one hundred and twenty inches) per annum. The rocky western coast is reef-bound and dangerous to approach, but on the eastern side there are several safe harbours at the mouths of rivers. The main settlement is at Muara-Siberut and this was where we arrived, going ashore in Helmut's rubber dinghy which we inflated on the deck of our steamer. Some canoes came out from the shore as soon as we anchored and helped us ferry ourselves and our equipment ashore. We made quite a large party since Helmut's attractive wife, Helga, and the four eldest of his five children, had all come with us. It was touching to see how happy the whole Buchholz family were to be back in Siberut. The parents had spent eight years there and all the children had been born on the island.

Helmut Buchholz originally went to the island of Siberut as a Protestant missionary working for a German fundamentalist sect. During his time there, he came to disagree with most of the methods and objectives of his mission. He grew to appreciate the significance and the value of traditional cultural traits as well as observing the negative effects of measures being taken in the name of progress. He and his wife are the only non-islanders to speak the Mentawai language fluently and we were shortly to see how loved and trusted they both were by the islanders. He began to worry more about the physical welfare of the islanders than about their spiritual conversion to his sect's particular form of Christianity. He saw how they were fought over and abused simply because they were strange and little known and he saw that, in the long run, what was happening would destroy them.

Inevitably, these views brought him into conflict with the mission and, after some bitter arguments, during which his colleagues turned on him, fabricating stories about him and trying to have him recalled to Germany, he eventually resigned from the mission and took a job on the mainland working for the World Bank. What impressed me most about him was that he had come through this difficult and agonizing time without losing his faith or his energy and enthusiasm. He now wanted more than ever to help the Mentawaians and firmly believed that, given the chance, he could do so. We could not possibly have had a wiser or more capable guide and companion.

The extent of Helmut's break with his mission was forcibly demonstrated to us soon after our arrival. We went about a quarter of a mile up the river past the little Malay town of Muara-Siberut at the mouth of the river to the small mission town where everything is carefully demarcated between the Roman Catholics, the Protestants, police and the military. There we carried our things to the Roman Catholic mission where Helmut told us with a twinkle in his eye not only was the company much more congenial but the food was a lot better than we would find anywhere else. He was, of course, absolutely right. We were soon being fussed over by half a dozen voluble and charming Italian priests and nuns. Bleary and dishevelled after the sixteen hours spent on deck during the crossing, we could scarcely believe our eyes when one of the nuns, dressed in T-shirt and jeans, thrust generous glasses of brandy into our hands. Although the sun was barely up, she insisted, quite rightly, that this was exactly what we needed.

After we had bathed and settled in, we sat and talked to the priests and to a zoologist who was doing research on the island and had made a special visit to the mission to meet me. They showed us cuttings from a recent Sumatran newspaper which had indicated a new campaign to change the Mentawai people and their way of life. A few years previously the situation had been very bad. Virtual purges had been undertaken against the Mentawaians in an effort to Islamize them. Pigs had been shot so that the people could not go on living in the jungle, their houses had been burnt down and those who had refused to move to the new villages had been punished. On one occasion, all the men from a wide area had been invited to a feast by the police. When they had arrived at the police post in the north of the island, they had been told to leave their weapons outside the village and to assemble in the centre. Then they had been surrounded by armed policemen who had told them that if they tried to run away they would be shot. Their long plaited hair which, in some cases, reached down to their waists, had then been cut off and taken away, it was suggested, for sale in Singapore.

In the south, similar things had happened in the name of Christianity with the traditional communal long houses being burnt down and the people being virtually terrorized into subjection. In both cases, the worst offenders had themselves been Mentawai islanders who had achieved positions of authority, one as a policeman, the other as a Christian missionary.

Then, for the last couple of years, things had been a little better and this was largely due to Helmut Buchholz's intercession with the governor of West Sumatra who had officially confirmed that the Mentawaians had a right to practise their traditional way of life. But now the cuttings we were shown featured pictures of bare-breasted Mentawai women who, it was affirmed, were ignorant savages. All this, the article continued, was to be changed, so that within a year the people would be civilized.

Everyone felt that this was a very dangerous development The missionaries agreed that the question of clothes was a difficult one because if you move too quickly the people would get colds and get weak, not knowing about washing them. On the other hand, they felt that they must have clothes to go into the town and deal with outsiders. One of the priests said, 'Before anybody came to Siberut the people were naked and strong, now they are clothed but weak and diseased. The children here must work in the mission school during the morning and in the government school in the afternoon. When will they play? When will they learn how to live and about the background of their family and their country?' Another answered, 'All these rules and plans are generated in offices with people who have no direct experience in the field. The Mentawaians are much more primitive than is generally realized and need a great deal of care and gentle attention before they will be able to cope on equal terms with the exploitative situation that surrounds them. We must go slowly, slowly, slowly.'

This was exactly what I was always hearing in Brazil but it was also something that nobody ever did anything about.

How do I give an impression of Siberut? We saw and heard so much and came away so dazed and filled with affection and a desire to help the Mentawaians that, unless I am careful, I will sound disgustingly sentimental. Both Marika and I feel unashamedly romantic about these people. The

Indians of Xingu in Brazil affected us in the same way, but there our romantic feelings were endorsed by many others who had lived and worked and been captivated. Only one anthropologist, Dr Reimar Schefold from Holland, has worked in Siberut and he left at a time when things were going badly and the outlook was bleak. His view was that the timber concessions recently granted by the Indonesian government to several foreign firms would seal the fate of the peoples' culture. During his two years on the island several groups had been forcibly moved to the coast where they had succumbed to disorientation and boredom. The rapid change from a full cultural life with ceremonies which often lasted for months on end, when each member of the clan had been able to give full rein to his creative capacities, to a 'modern', work-specialization régime had shocked and depressed him. The police had been active, treating tattooing, long hair and the observance of their traditional religious rites as criminal acts and punishing offenders. Only those living in sufficient isolation in the interior to be beyond the reach of the police had so far avoided such forced changes. If lumber companies now planned to extract the timber from these areas, the police would follow and they too would be forced to move. He had given me generous help and advice but had not been optimistic and so I had expected to find a depressed and bored detribalized society.

Thanks to Helmut Buchholz we were able to visit groups in the interior of the island who had not been abused and were still proud and independent. Thanks too to Helmut, the people we saw near the coast had, to a large extent, regained their pride and their confidence and had shown a remarkable ability to recover from the shocks inflicted on them. Helmut knows Siberut better than any other non-Mentawaian. Through him, we were able to talk with the people we met and understand what we saw. Just as the Indians of Xingu would have surely scattered and died without the help and friendship of the Villas Boas brothers (see

A Question of Survival), so I believe Helmut alone holds the key to the future of the Mentawaians of Siberut.

Within minutes of our arrival, the Buchholz children had vanished. Although they had been away for six months, they made it clear that this was their home, greeting friends instantly and running off with them without a backward glance. Helga decided to stay at the mission and try to keep a maternal eye on them while Helmut, Marika and I set off up the Sabirut river in a canoe which he had made himself and left behind pulled up on the bank. At first, we used a borrowed outboard motor but after turning up the Sarereiket river, we met shallows and rapids where frequently we had to wade waist-deep, pushing the boat against the strong current.

Men and women called to us from the bank. *'Ana leu ita'*, 'We are here together', the Mentawai greeting and asked us to stay with them. *'Kaipa?'* 'Where are you coming from?', they shouted, pointing downstream. *'Ka monga,'* replied Helmut. 'From the mouth of the river.' *'Kaipa?'* again, pointing upstream. 'Where are you going?' 'To the Sakaliou,' called Helmut, and they looked sad that we were on our way to another clan and would not be stopping with them. *'Moile, moile,'* the lovely Mentawai expression, meaning literally 'Slowly, slowly', but in reality much more like 'Take it easy, what's the hurry?' or 'Go in peace', floated after us. Every now and then, we passed neat little rows of logs tied together to make a raft moored to the shore. This was sago, used mostly as pig food, but also the staple human diet. Sago palms grow wild and take about eight to twelve years to reach maturity. Then, when the main stem is cut down and chopped into lengths, new shoots grow from the stump, an apparently almost everlasting cycle.

Every bit of land on Siberut belongs to some individual or clan and the boundaries are well-known and established. Every coconut palm belongs to someone too, although not necessarily the owner of the soil since these valuable trees are often used as exchange goods in bride payments or as compensation for damages such as adultery. Hunting, however, is permissible on other people's land, but even in the depths of the jungle it is always quite clear in every hunter's mind whose land he is on.

We stopped at midday at a place called Sabokolo. Wading ashore on Siberut rivers for the first time was an unfamiliar and uncomfortable experience as the mud was knee-deep and clinging. Then, once the bank had been climbed, the path to the house consisted of precarious little poles laid end to end across the mud and over gullies. The main platform of the house, on stilts and with some pigs rooting underneath, was reached by a log notched on one side so that it can be turned over at night to stop animals climbing up.

This was the first of many *umas* or clan houses we were to see and we were immediately impressed, as we were to be again and again, by how beautifully and well they were built, simply from wood and palm thatch. In the front was a wide veranda, open on three sides, where a few men and women were sitting, repairing arrows and making fishing lines. Behind was a large, wide room with a wooden dancing floor in the centre where ceremonies and celebrations took place, and further back still stretching away into the darkness were the cooking fires and sleeping places for families. The wooden uprights and plank walls, all made with axes, never with saws, were covered in bas-relief carvings of crocodiles, gibbons, storks, deer, and other animals. From the rafters hung a mass of objects looking like the roof of a sorcerer's den. Skulls of pigs and monkeys, deer's antlers and bones; big black gongs and iron pots representing wealth; drums, musical instruments, feathers and bows and arrows, as well as bundles of herbs and dried food, pickling over the big central fire, built on sand and flat stones.

At Sabokolo, there were three particularly large crocodile skulls. Helmut said he had himself seen crocodiles over four metres long on Siberut, but that the people only hunt them when they kill someone. Then they will go on hunting until they find one with clothes or other human remains in its belly. He also told us he had seen an exceptionally large python on the island. Without its head, which had been cut off, it had measured nine metres sixty centimetres. Pythons are common and rather a nuisance because they kill the chickens and an occasional small pig, but they are not regarded as a danger to man. There is a common variety of small green snake which is venomous but not deadly and we hardly met a man who could not show us a scar or two where he had been bitten. On the other hand, we heard of no one who had survived the bite of the cobra, but we were assured that they will only attack when they have young.

We were given sago, roasted young in long, thin shoots and wrapped in its own leaves. Also, sugar cane was cut for us to chew and coconuts were pierced so we could drink the water and then cracked open and a sliver of wood cut off to make a spoon for eating the soft food inside.

The Mentawai people reminded me a lot of the Choco Indians in Panama and Colombia with whom I had spent some time the year before. They had the same peaceful approach to arrivals and departures; no great performance of shouting and handshakes. They liked to sit quietly and discuss things, the men preferring to wear bark loincloths which they said were more comfortable than cloth ones. The women normally only wore a sarong, although nearer the coast and where mission schools had been established, all, even little girls of nine or ten, wore off-white brassières, which looked incongruous. Many of the men had intricate tattoos all over their bodies. Although this was forbidden for a time, it was now coming back again and we saw several who had had their modern names given to them by a missionary, tattooed on their forearms. Men, women and children wore flowers in their hair or stuck in bead headbands around their foreheads. All had bright, inquisitive eyes, pale brown skin and very ready, fresh smiles.

* * *

In the evening, we came to a tiny tributary called the Bat Kaliou. When the river is high, one can sometimes paddle a canoe up this, but as we had found to our cost, the water was very low and we had been wading and pushing for most of the last few hours, only using the motor between shallows. Some people came out of the jungle as we arrived. The women and girls were dressed from head to knee in banana leaves and grass skirts. When they saw Helmut, they laughed and ran to greet us. They looked sheepish when he asked them why they were so over-dressed. It turned out that, hearing our motor in the distance, they assumed it must be the Catholic priests passing or perhaps even the military coming to inspect them and having no clothes with them as they were out fishing, had hurriedly made these garments from available material. They offered to help us carry our possessions inland to the Sakaliou *uma* which lay about a mile away, deliberately hidden in the forest from those who would otherwise try to make them move to the coast. Helmut said we must take the petrol cans too. 'Mentawaians would never take everything', he said. 'Nor indeed would they steal an object, but each one who passes on the river would take just a little petrol, knowing that we wouldn't grudge them that and when we returned there would be almost none left.'

Walking to the *uma* was not easy. The ground was wet and the mud deep. Thin poles, often roughly propped two or three feet above the ground, broke under our weight and were very slippery. Marika found it particularly difficult to keep her balance and made slow progress. '*Moile, moile*', the Mentawaians called, solicitously giving her a hand and showing her the best way. I teased her, saying they had given her this name because she was so excessively slow. In fact, all they meant was, 'There's no hurry, take your time'. It took a long time, but at last we arrived to find a really splendid *uma*, with a little stream, the upper part of the Bat Kaliou. Here, we bathed our bruised and bleeding feet and washed off the mud of our many falls before going up the notched pole to the main platform.

I had first heard about Siberut from Sir Peter Scott, one of Survival International's sponsors, to whom I had written, saying I was planning to go to Indonesia and could he suggest any areas of interest. He had replied enthusiastically, telling me that there were several rare species of primates known to live on the island, especially the pygmy gibbon (*Hylobates klossi*) as well as macaques and langurs. The International Union for Conservation of Nature and Natural Resources (IUCN) was interested in setting up a reserve there for the protection of these and other species and had recently sent a mission out to investigate the possibilities. They too had been guided by Helmut and had spoken highly of his abilities.

The problem is that, as well as growing sago, tubers, bananas and coconuts, the Mentawai people are hunters. Their only domesticated animals are pigs and chickens and these are normally only eaten on special occasions, their killing being a matter for ritual and the placating of spirits. The rest of their diet is provided by hunting and fishing and, since monkeys and gibbons are among the easiest game to hunt, it follows that as the human population increases their numbers are likely to suffer. Recently, in some of the more densely populated areas, villagers, hungry for meat, had banded together to organize drives in the course of which every mammal and bird was killed, leaving behind, in the case of one peninsula, an almost total absence of edible game. A temporary answer, at least from the wildlife point of view, seemed to be the establishment of a restricted area of the interior, in which hunting would be prohibited while allowing logging operations to continue up to its boundaries. The cooperation of the Indonesian government would be needed in the setting up, policing and administration of such a reserve, the Mentawaians would have to be prevented from entering it and stricter rules to control the activities of the expatriate timber workers would have to be agreed, but on the face of it the plan seemed to make sense. During long talks, interpreted by Helmut, with the clan Sakaliou and others, I was to begin to realize that unfortunately the concept of a reserve was neither practicable nor desirable when applied to the island of Siberut.

We sat cross-legged on the split bamboo floor of the *uma,* smoking and eating sago, plantains and pork and dropping scraps through the cracks to the pigs penned below. About thirty members of the clan gathered round us in the darkness, relieved only by the flickering light of a few wicks burning in oil, and listened intently as Helmut questioned them about what had been happening since he was last there. Apart from him, we were the first outsiders they had ever allowed to visit them and it was clear that they admired and respected him. There was a most moving moment when the *Kerei,* or chief witch doctor, arrived late the first evening. He and Helmut, who is normally the most undemonstrative of men, stood in silence for a long time, clasped in each other's arms, and, in the Mentawai way, stroked each other's shoulders with deep affection. Both were noticeably moved at meeting again.

Later still, they began to talk about us and what our purpose was in being there. Helmut relayed questions from them to me which were often loaded and difficult to answer. I felt myself in the presence of a highly intelligent and alert audience who missed very little of what was going on, even when Helmut and I were speaking German together or Marika and I, English. They knew very well the direction their questions were leading and I did not so I had to be careful about what I said.

'Do you like it here on the Bat Kaliou?'. Of course, I replied, 'Yes'.

'Would you prefer to live in Muara-Siberut?' 'No!'

'Where is your home?' 'Far away across many seas in a place called Cornwall.'

'Would you rather be living here or there?' 'Here.'

'Well, why don't you?' This required a long and rather complicated reply about how I too had my clan and family and I could not bring all of them to live there too. But they knew they had caught me out and we laughed together. We seemed to have been accepted by them, and liked not just because we were Helmut's friends but for ourselves, and perhaps also because we had been pretty generous with tobacco and cigarettes.

Then Helmut brought up the subject of a wildlife reserve, explaining that there were people who felt that some of the animals, in particular the gibbons, were important, perhaps more important than people and should be protected. Unfortunately, they misunderstood him and thought that I was one of these people and that this idea had emanated from me. The change in atmosphere was electric and frightening. Suddenly, I could catch no one's eye and I actually felt that we were in danger. A man in the shadows at the back shouted, 'If he thinks that way, he should leave the *uma* now!' Helmut explained that my concern was for them, but that there were people who felt this way and believed that the Mentawaians should be prevented from hunting in certain areas. There was a long period of shocked silence after this. The shock was quite palpable as though there had been an explosion. Then, 'Who are these people who feel this way? Are they human or are they apes themselves?'

'Well, if they feel like that, they should go and live in the trees themselves!'

'Preferably on the Butet Elágat!'

This last, I gathered, rather coarse reference to a particular type of tree brought laughter and the atmosphere lightened.

But Helmut persevered. 'If such a reserve were created and the police, the government, the missionaries and I myself, all said that you should not go there and that that area, the whole valley perhaps, was not to be hunted, what would you do?'

The answer came back emphatically and without hesitation. 'We would go and hunt there. This is our land we have always hunted and no one will stop us doing that.'

'But if you had enough food here—fish, for example—would you still go hunting?'

Again I was surprised by the speed and certainty of the reply. 'Of course not; fishing is much easier and fish is better to eat. If there were plenty of fish, we would not need to hunt except sometimes on special occasions and for special rituals. But fish is scarce and so we have to hunt.'

Helmut then explained to them an idea he has to introduce a type of fish from the mainland which would live in the shallow ponds where they plant cassava and which grow very quickly on a diet of cassava leaves. They readily grasped the idea and accepted Helmut's word that such a scheme might be possible. He has already helped several clans by improving their fishing techniques, introducing nets and persuading them not to use poison which destroy all the fish so that it takes a long time for the fishing to be any good again.

Increasing the number of pigs and chickens would not help a lot, as these are not normally eaten, except at ceremonies. Another source of protein is needed in addition to these.

This conversation convinced me that if a wildlife reserve were to be designated anywhere on the island, it would be impossible to police and the Mentawai people would strongly oppose it.

It was now my turn to ask questions. 'How is your life now compared to a few years ago?'

'Much better,' they replied. 'Then we lived on the river and things were very bad. The police came and made us cut our hair and burned our bead headbands. Now we have moved away from the river and the police have never been here. Also Helmut brought us new beads last year and now we have made new bands.'

They showed us some, taking them from their heads or off the children. Bright, attractive patterns and colourful designs. I asked which colours they liked best and they answered as a group, calling from different parts of the house, 'Bright red', 'Light green—not dark', 'Dark blue', 'Clear white—not black'. Helmut explained, 'These people were much cleverer than the Sakuddai (the people the anthropologist Reimar Schefold lived with). Instead of making a demonstration and fighting authority, they simply let their house by the river fall down and built a new one somewhere inland. When asked what they have in there, they simply say there are just a few pigs and that they cut wood. No missionaries have been to this *uma* either and I think you would agree that it is a long enough walk to deter most outsiders.' We looked at our feet and agreed.

He went on, 'You have seen these beautiful headbands they wear. When I first came to Siberut, there were very few of these being worn and I found out that this was because the police had taken them away and burnt them. I asked the police why they had done this and they said, "Because they are primitive." This made me angry and I replied, "You are the primitive ones, not realizing that a thing is beautiful when you see it." I went to the governor and asked if there was a law against wearing headbands. He said, "No" and reprimanded the police. It so happened that the chief of police on the island at that time was the brother-in-law of my colleague, the Protestant preacher, and they were not amused. Nor did they think it funny when I arrived back the next day with fifty-five kilos of beads I had bought with my own money. But the people appreciated it and now you see headbands everywhere on the island.'

I asked the Sakaliou what they wanted most and after a short consultation among themselves, they answered as follows, 'We need mosquito nets most as these we cannot make. Also we would like to have lots of beads and other pretty things to wear as ornaments, little bells which we can use in our magic ceremonies, and of course gongs are valuable. Besides this we wish firstly that the police would not try to stop our world; secondly, that our medicine should be good; and thirdly, that our religion should be strong. We say all this *only* because Helmut asks for you. To anyone else, we would be afraid and we would say that we need nothing.'

It was midnight by this time which is very late indeed in the tropics and we were dropping with exhaustion after a long, hard day. Marika and I laid out our sleeping bags side by side and put up our large military mosquito net over them both. This was examined and discussed with great interest, and Helmut explained that not only was its quality being admired and the possibility of its use as a fishing net, since it was so strongly made, but also concern was being expressed about our sleeping arrangements. Men and women never sleep together in the *umas* but make love in the jungle or in their own individual huts away near their plantations. We assured everyone that our intention was simply to share the mosquito net and nothing more. This, it was decided, would be tolerated, although it was made fairly clear that we were acting in rather bad taste.

The pigs were fed at dawn. Whole trunks of sago palms were simply rolled off the platform of the *uma* into the mud below where the pigs devoured them completely. Other logs were cut open for the chickens who stood on them in a row like factory hens at feeding time and wasted nothing. Obviously, it was a satisfactory diet as the pigs were quite astonishingly fat. This is the way the Mentawaians like them although they would not appeal to a European pork butcher, having a ratio of fat to lean meat of about four to one.

Feeding time churned up the mud below the *uma* but later it rained and the little stream rose until the whole area was flooded and washed clean by the water which then dropped, allowing us to walk down the pole path again to the river. We went upstream some way and then walked up a long, rocky riverbed to see a waterfall at a place called Kulukubu which Helmut said was the highest on Siberut and had never been seen by outsiders or photographed before. It fell a sheer hundred feet into a deep pool of clear water, silencing the tropical din with its rushing and wetting the surrounding vegetation with spray. There is a legend that two women were fishing at the top and one fell near the edge. The other went to help her and both were swept over and drowned. Now sometimes their hands are seen above the water, a bad omen foretelling disaster.

Further up the main river, we visited Matobak, a resettlement village, officially created by the police. Later, on the coast, we were to see another such development and there are many more scattered around the island. Straight rows of twenty to thirty box-like houses three metres square had been put up and the people encouraged to move into them. Almost none had stayed, the rest politely saying that they made useful chicken houses and stores for pig food. If they heard that the police were going to inspect them, they would come and stand in front of their individual huts before returning to their *umas* hidden in the jungle. The dead, abandoned atmosphere of these 'model' villages was very depressing and contrasted sharply with the vitality of the large communal houses. In most places the people were afraid to build new *umas* or repair the old ones since this would make the police lose face and cause trouble. Money had been provided by the government for these housing projects, but since the Mentawaians had been ordered to build them themselves and would then not dream of living in them, they received no benefit, Meanwhile, the funds conveniently disappeared somewhere in the chain of command. However, near Matobak, we were encouraged to find two beautiful new *umas* being built. One was twenty metres long and nearly finished. Everything had been done with great care and skill. The ends of the roof beams were finely carved, the interweaving of the palm-leaf thatch made delightful patterns. The walls were covered with bas-reliefs of animals and birds and the bamboo floors, uprights, railings and other details, were all superbly finished. Helmut was delighted as it takes eight months to build an *uma* and the fine workmanship showed that, not only were the police being less strict and allowing the people to live in their own style, but also that the culture, far from being dead, was flourishing. We all admired the workmanship and congratulated the builders, agreeing that, although as they meet the threat of outside interference, the Mentawaians' way of life is changing and they certainly need help to adapt, to suggest that they do not know how to build houses is absurd.

Wherever we stayed the night, a feast was laid on in Helmut's honour and to welcome him back. Once this was combined with a ceremony to drive away bad spirits from a sick child. The *Kerei* sat in the centre, colourfully draped with strings of beads, wreaths of flowers and bunches of feathers. On his arms were brass bangles and with his right hand he insistently jangled a small silver bell. In front of him was a bowl of red and white hibiscus blooms and a little box containing beads, bottles, pieces of cloth and other small objects. A white cockerel with a bright red comb was brought and put in his hands. It lay quite still while he stroked and talked to it as it stared up at him with sharp, beady eyes. Then he carried it round the *uma*, holding it over each person's head, chanting and blessing them. He came to us and I asked what he had said. 'Go away bad spirits from these good people', Helmut translated, adding that outsiders were not usually honoured in this way.

More chickens were brought and a pig was tied up outside. Later, they were slaughtered one by one but even while the chickens' necks were being wrung and the pig's throat cut, the *Kerei* stroked them and talked to them, explaining that this was being done only because the people were hungry and needed to eat. He apologized to their spirits for the necessity of disturbing them and strangely enough the animals lay quiet and did not struggle. While the carcasses were being prepared for cooking, the *Kerei* examined the entrails, carefully parting them and searching for omens. Everyone sat quietly, waiting for the verdict and then laughed with relief and began to chatter happily when he said that all was well and the child would live. The food was placed in a large basin and a wooden bowl of water brought to us to wash our hands in. Then we all dipped in, pulling out the rather fatty morsels and passing the specially delicious bits to each other. As well as the pork and chicken, the bowl contained pieces of bony fish and whole crayfish caught in the river. Pigs' trotters were on a big leaf and boiled green ferns made an excellent vegetable course. A steaming bowl of sago appeared, rather like a cross between fried rice and Brazilian *farinha* and we learnt to roll it between our fingers before popping it into our mouths. The children scrambled everywhere, at first avoiding us and peering around the adults with huge, luminous eyes. Gradually they became braver, reaching out to touch us and finally, when they discovered we would not bite, becoming a menace as they climbed all over us, examining everything but taking nothing. The rather savage hunting dogs skulked in the shadows, darting in to grab scraps and being rather half-heartedly shooed away from time to time. When they became too aggressive, an old woman was sent out of the *uma* and returned after a few minutes with a branch covered with leaves which she handed to one of the men. When the next dog approached, he leant forward and stroked it on the back with the branch. A few seconds later, the dog bounded off the platform and disappeared howling into the night. Closer inspection revealed that under the leaves were clusters of small black ants which bit viciously. From then on, merely raising the branch was enough to keep the dogs at bay.

The Mentawaians have two ancient myths about their origin. We found both strangely familiar and decided that one should be called the Darwin myth and the other the Cinderella Oedipus myth. According to the first, there were once only gibbons living in the trees. But they bred rapidly and, without enemies, became too many, so that one day some had to come down and live on the ground. From these, in time, came people. The second goes as follows. Once upon a time, there was a shipwreck off the coast of northern Siberut. Only a pregnant woman made it ashore and lived. She had a son and when he grew up she said he must go out into the world and search for a wife. She gave him a ring and said that when he found a woman whom it fitted, he should marry her. He travelled for several years but found no one with a finger of the right size. At last he returned to Siberut but his mother and he did not know each other. The ring fitted, they were married and became the ancestors of all the people on the island.

Probably the gravest threat to the Mentawaians is the presence of several foreign lumber companies exploiting the island's timber. I visited one of the Philippino camps, walking inland from a beach where Helmut and Helga wept to see the total destruction of a place they said had once been the most beautiful spot on the island. An idyllic coral reef and sandy beach where they used to picnic had been totally destroyed by bulldozers and dynamite to make a landing stage. Huge tree-trunks lay strewn around the bay. Struggling knee- to waist-deep in horrible clinging mud and bare red earth, we made our way for mile after mile through a nightmare landscape which looked as though it had been hit by a gigantic bomb. Although the loggers are only allowed to export trees over sixty centimetres in girth, this does not unfortunately mean that the rest of the environment is left undisturbed. The crawler tractors have to reach the trees and to do so they have to make roads. Much of the rest of the vegetation is smashed in the process and since the roads soon turn to rivers and become impassable, while lakes form in the hollows making new roads necessary, little is left standing except for a few trees of slightly under sixty centimetres across, rising up out of the mud. The soil is very weak and leaches rapidly under the immense rainfall so that the destruction is permanent.

We then struggled back through the mud and the undergrowth to the Philippino camp on the beach where we saw a large fish which had quite clearly been dynamited. Only the lumber operatives have access to dynamite and apparently they use it quite often in this illegal and wasteful way of fishing. They also contribute to the meat shortage legitimately by buying chickens from the islanders. However, these are not the worst impacts of the timber businesses on Siberut. Rather they come from the effect which the labour gangs have upon the indigenous people. This causes the breakdown of their society through prostitution, drink, unfamiliar work patterns and movement from clan houses to villages or labour camps. With these changes, the taboos against hunting are removed and the total eradication of species of wildlife becomes possible. I also heard that quite large numbers of gibbons had been exported secretly to Singapore in timber ships and sold there to dealers.

Prostitution and the introduction of venereal diseases are becoming serious problems. We heard several stories of the police selling Mentawaian girls to the Philippino workers as well as importing Javanese girls who were sold outright for one hundred pounds each. One of the Mentawai who had been procured by the previous Mayor of Siberut—her name was Simainga and she came from Katurai—lived permanently on the Philippino ship, the *Yesmak*, which was moored offshore and from time to time brought supplies from Padang. Other girls had been brought from villages in the interior by the police and sold to one of the camps. A Catholic teacher at Muara-Siberut gave an example of a recent and unpunished case of rape. 'Four women were fishing on the coast with nets when some Philippinos arrived by boat, caught them and raped them. They told their husbands what had happened, even naming one of the men whom they knew. When they all went to the police to complain, they were told that since there were no non-Mentawaian witnesses, there was no proof and nothing could be done about it. When the men went to the camp and asked the Philippinos themselves to admit what they had done, the police arrived and fired their guns to frighten the Mentawaians away. As a result, the islanders are now afraid to go near the lumber camps or work for them, so that there is a labour shortage.'

Among the Mentawaians, there are a great many taboos and customs about sex. Some of these have the effect of keeping down the population since sexual intercourse is prohibited for several weeks before ceremonies and at certain times of year. For example, sex is taboo while the pigs are breeding. Once all the sows are seen to have been mated by the boars, all the boars are castrated and that particular taboo is lifted until the subsequent brood of young pigs is old enough to breed again. When adultery occurs—or is discovered—the man in the case has to pay substantial compensation in the form of pigs and chickens or even land or coconut palms. These customs cannot be enforced against the Philippinos, which has made the islanders very angry. Gonorrhoea first occurred on the island in 1971 and has since spread rapidly. In fact, in some clans, it has developed so fast that the good Catholic nuns believed, in their innocence, that it must have been transmitted by the water. The Mentawaians, who know very well how they got it, are ashamed to go to the mission so that the disease is in danger of sweeping over the whole island. Helmut appealed to the Governor, who sent two Indonesian doctors but they were afraid to go into the interior and reported that they had diagnosed no cases of venereal diseases.

The question of missionaries and education is rather more difficult to assess. Undoubtedly, many of the missionaries are good people who genuinely wish to help the Mentawaians and teach them to cope with the modern world. The trouble is that there are, as is so often the case, too many of them competing with each other and saying different things. Four main beliefs are actively preached on the island; Baha'i which is proscribed but apparently very strong in the region, Islam, Roman Catholicism and Protestantism. It is one of the tragedies of a situation like that to be found on Siberut that the tremendous energy devoted to missionary work, appears to arise out of the challenge presented by a strange and fascinating people. Everybody fights over them and tries to alter them to their own particular way of thinking, creating confusion in the people's minds while combining to disrupt their own culture and beliefs. Once these are effectively destroyed and the people have become a sad, depressed and bored social problem, living in shanty towns around the coast, one has a nasty feeling that most of the missionaries will move on to fresh fields. Meanwhile, the children being taught in the rival schools have learnt to mistrust each other while, at the same time, losing the opportunity to learn about their own traditions and identity.

Helmut was very honest with us about his own change of attitude towards these difficulties. Although never a fanatic, he had been a missionary and one of the most impressive things about him was the way he had managed to survive the traumatic break with his sect without losing his own faith. His views had simply altered through experience and observation. He now believed that it was a mistake to attempt to change the Mentawaians, either by criticism or by force, but rather to let them realize in their own time that certain changes were necessary and would help them to survive and prosper. This attitude was surprisingly convincing when it came to the question of conservation on the island, the issue which had first brought it to my attention. The example of the other islands in the Mentawai group, where almost all the people are settled in towns and have, through hunger, ruthlessly destroyed most of the wildlife, demonstrated that a scattered population with an economy based on fishing, farming and periodic hunting, could paradoxically and with a little help represent a safeguard rather than a threat to the animals. The Mentawaians use only bows and arrows. None have rifles yet. Moreover, they are not enthusiastic hunters and killers of wild animals, doing so only for food and in no sense for sport. Hunting is surrounded by many taboos and much time is spent apologizing to the spirits of the animals to be hunted for the necessity of killing them and explaining that it is only because they are hungry. The best way, therefore, to help the wildlife and especially the primate population of Siberut, is to help the Mentawai people themselves to improve both their existing sources of domestic animal protein (pigs and chickens) as well as introducing fish nets and teaching them more sophisticated methods of benefiting from the rich rivers and coastal waters while, at the same time, seeking new sources of protein.

As a result, I proposed to the International Union for Conservation of Nature and Natural Resources (IUCN) and the World Wildlife Fund, that in cooperation with Survival International, the funds planned to be used for a wildlife reserve should be applied to financing Helmut Buchholz to return to the island and maintaining him there. By improving the agricultural, animal husbandry and fishing techniques of the Mentawai people, he would gradually reduce their need to hunt and so protect the island's threatened species. At the same time, he would be in a strong position to make sure that the existing prohibitions against others hunting on the island were enforced, while representing the people's interests as the pressures upon them inevitably increase. I became fully convinced that no programme of research nor yet the establishment of reserves and regulations, could achieve half as much as this plan and I hope that by the time this book is published it may have been implemented. Unfortunately, after initial enthusiasm, certain sections of the conservation world—not including, I am glad to say, Sir Peter Scott—have found the whole idea rather too novel for their taste so that at present the future of Siberut is uncertain. Helmut's current contract in Sumatra expires soon and, if he then has to return to Europe, a unique opportunity will, I believe, have been lost.

Kubu

❧

After a stormy crossing back to the mainland of Sumatra, we spent two very pleasant days in the Bukittinggi hills with the Buchholz family. This gave us a chance to wash our clothes and rest. We also had a glimpse of the fiercely Muslim Minangkabau people with their elegant traditional houses now mostly roofed in corrugated iron, as well as the romantic hills and valleys in which they live. High and sometimes active volcanoes tower above rocky gorges coated with luxuriant tropical vegetation, leading down to the flat and fertile coastal plain.

Marika, Helmut and I then flew to Palembang in southern Sumatra, a most uninspiring oil town with one long main street and a ridiculous, huge bridge built by the Japanese as compensation after the war. The bridge has a central section which can be lifted on two giant towers in order to let ships pass through. This was demonstrated in 1948 at the official opening of the bridge. But since the charge is about one hundred and fifty pounds for each ship to pass through and there is nothing up the Palembang river to attract large ships, it has never happened since. The oil refineries and other installations are all downstream of the bridge and that is where the tankers and supply ships tie up. There too is the company town, with houses, hotels and clubs for the oil technicians and executives, so that the centre of Palembang is almost free of Europeans. The rather irritating habit of young Indonesian males to follow Europeans—and particularly blonde females—down the street shouting, 'Hi, mister! What you want, mister?' is particularly prevalent there. Helmut has an excellent repertoire of Indonesian swear words and his tendency to grab the most aggressive youth if he came too close and jostled us and hold him up to public shame by asking him where he had learnt to behave in such an uncultured way, was most effective in putting a stop to it as well as creating a much more friendly atmosphere, combining good humour and even hilarity with respect and sage expressions of agreement from the older generation of passers-by. However, to achieve this a fluent command of Indonesian is required and we were as glad of his company in towns as we had been in the jungle. Through spending so much time with him and speaking German since his English was poor, my own Indonesian, which later became passable, had not had much chance to develop.

We stayed in a Chinese hotel which Marika, preferring the two extremes of civilized luxury or basic jungle life, regarded as the worst of both worlds. The dim lights only worked intermittently, the floors and walls were filthy. There was no way of reducing or even fanning the stuffy heat and from the single cold tap rusty brown water trickled incessantly. Surprisingly the passage lights came on strongly at midnight and remained shining through the ragged wire cage around our room for the rest of the night. A couple of hours before dawn some of the other residents began to get up accompanying their ablutions with a crescendo of hawking and spitting.

At Djambi, where the World Bank/Bonn University project had its headquarters, Helmut again became a dynamo of organizational energy. Dumping us at the project house where we found a polyglot mixture of German, French, Indonesian, English and other nationalities, some with wives, trying rather irritably to communicate in blended languages, he went off to 'fix' what would undoubtedly have taken us days and cost a fortune on our own. An hour later he was back with a beaten-up Willys jeep, information on the whereabouts of a Kubu group and a letter from a local prince to the head man of the village nearest to them. His main disappointment was that no fuel had arrived for the helicopter which the project director had generously promised us and which would have taken us fast and in comfort much further into Kubu country. The jeep would only be able to go some of the way and when we met the swamps and network of small rivers behind which the Kubu live, we would have to walk. Explaining this, he turned ruefully towards Marika, saying that he doubted if she would be able to make it as we would have to travel very fast through worse country even than Siberut. He could not afford to spend the time going slowly and risking delays as he had to be back at work on the following Monday (it was then Saturday morning), having already taken two weeks off work to come to Siberut with us. Before I began to translate this, Marika had guessed what it was all about. Although bitterly disappointed and ready to try anything, she realized that there was no time for argument.

'I'll fly to Jakarta tomorrow and wait for you there. We're supposed to be lunching with the ambassador on Tuesday. If you do get stuck or carried away, at least I can explain why you're not there!'

At this, Helmut looked profoundly relieved and congratulated me on having such an understanding wife, saying that until that moment he had always thought his own Helga was unique in this respect.

Within minutes, it was all settled and taking only one knapsack with mosquito nets, sleeping bags, cameras and film, we clattered off up the rough earth road leading west out of Djambi. We stopped at a village market and bought tobacco for the Kubu before turning off the road and bumping along a track to the south. At first, we passed several mechanical oil dippers, sinister in their unmanned isolation as they bobbed regularly up and down, pumping oil out of the ground and along pipelines to the storage tanks at Djambi. Then these thinned out and we reached the small thatched settlement of Pelempang. The head man, whose name was Maliki, turned out to be young and energetic in contrast to most of the other inhabitants who were taking their ease in patches of shade, giving the place the air of a Mexican *pueblo.* He was himself a Kubu and although he expressed doubts about our ability to reach our objective by nightfall, saying that we would probably have to sleep in the open, agreed to give it a try and come with us himself to show us the way. 'We will have to go very fast and you will be left behind but I will wait for you,' he said.

He had reckoned without Helmut who hoisted our possessions onto his shoulders, asked which path to follow and set off down it at a fast trot. We kept up this pace, about ten kilometres per hour, for the next three and a half hours, only stopping occasionally to wait for Maliki to catch up and tell us which way to go when the track forked. Taking it in turns to carry the bag, which became progressively heavier and soaked in sweat, we ran along dry, bare ground under high gallery forest, sloshed through muddy stretches of swamp tangled with the roots of trees growing out of the water and teetered across slippery fallen logs, bridging the deeper, meandering streams. The stops gave us a chance to flick the small, black leeches off our legs but also allowed the mosquitoes time to gather for concentrated attacks. As the sun began to set and the shadows to lengthen, we heard the characteristic whooping of gibbons and, for a time, a troop of pale brown langurs kept us company, crashing from one treetop to another in great, suicidal leaps. Helmut, who a few hours before, had been the very image of an efficient German businessman, dealing with airline tickets and officials, now ran barefoot like a teutonic Tarzan calling out the names of plants and birds and, from time to time, pausing to gather edible fruit to quench our thirst.

Just when every muscle was beginning to ache unbearably and I was wondering how much longer I could keep up the gruelling pace, we reached a delightful little river, flowing fast between high banks. It was one of those spots which remain forever imprinted in my mind so that whenever I think of the jungles of southern Sumatra, it is there I see first. An old tree, leaning out from the bank, provided a perfect jetty, and the fresh, clear water was so immediately inviting that we both tore off our filthy, soaking clothes and plunged in to lie submerged and cool beneath the surface. When Maliki arrived, he said that there should be a Kubu family nearby but he was not quite sure where as they were always moving about. We followed a faint track, littered with rotten logs. Beside one of these, I saw what at a first, unthinking glance looked to me like a baby lobster somehow transported a hundred miles from the nearest sea. It was dark, shining green and waved substantial claws in the air while its tail curved up menacingly. A scorpion, of course, but quite the largest I had ever seen, shown to measure well over eight inches by Helmut who put his bare foot down beside it and dismissed it as quite commonplace.

Darkness had almost fallen by the time we reached a well-made fence of stakes lashed tight together and designed to keep wild pigs away from the small cassava plantation within. In the centre of the clearing was a diminutive thatched hut on stilts which we reached by a rickety ladder to join the family group of shy and slender people sitting cross-legged on the veranda.

The Kubu are of a quite different racial origin from the surrounding Malay population and are thought to be the descendants of a mixture of early Veddoid and Negrito stock. The Veddoid peoples, named after the Vedda tribe of Ceylon, may have been one of the races to migrate through south-east Asia during the last Ice Age and to have reached Australia across the Sahul Shelf which then joined the island of New Guinea to the mainland. They may thus have contributed to the make-up of the Australian aborigines. They are usually hunters, with dark skins, long wavy hair and relatively long, narrow (dolichocephalic) heads. Although they are thought to have once been a widespread population they are now only found as remnant groups, usually amalgamated with other peoples, in Malaysia, Sumatra, Celebes and a few other islands. The Negritos, who are a small, sometimes pygmy race, are characterized by dark-brown or black woolly hair, yellowish-brown to black skin with generally thick lips, broad, flat noses and large, prominent eyes. Some authorities believe that they were an early Asian race driven south by subsequent populations while others maintain that the pygmies to be found in scattered areas from Africa to New Guinea, are simply modified representatives of the local general populace.

Little is known about the Kubu, their beliefs, culture or even their present numbers. They are shy hunter gatherers who roam the dense jungles, swamps and little rivers of south-east Sumatra in bands of twenty to thirty persons, avoiding contact with the surrounding population and resisting efforts to settle them. In the 1930s, the Dutch forced some of them to live in villages near the Malays and attempted to make them take up agriculture, but many left to return to a nomadic way of life. For a long time, contact with them only took place through 'silent trade' whereby goods for barter were left out by them at certain recognized spots and replaced with trade items so that no actual meeting occurred. This method of exchange has a long history having been practised in many parts of the world, particularly Africa where, according to Herodotus, the Carthaginians acquired gold from black tribes to the south in this way. It has also been reported from such widely separated areas as Lapland and New Guinea, from the Congo where the pygmies traded bananas for meat from the Bantu and in Ceylon where the Vedda obtained iron implements from Sinhalese smiths in return for game. Today it is rare, but a similar process is still used in Brazil, to establish contact with the remaining isolated tribes. Recently, several groups of Kubu have again been persuaded to settle and move away from a nomadic life to a more permanent agricultural system. However, even these seldom stay in one place for more than a year or so which accounted for our difficulty in tracking them down.

Two brothers who said their names were Denang and

Amin lived in this house with their respective families. They were related to Maliki and invited us to stay with them, offering us warm water, which they described as coffee, from an old kettle. It tasted to me indistinguishable from the river water we had drunk here and there on our way, but a few leaves had been infused into it and, as the evening drew on, I thought I could detect a faint aroma. We were given boiled cassava and little river fish to eat while Helmut tried out his Mentawai on them in preference to Indonesian as he had a theory that the two languages might have a common root. At first they denied even being able to speak the Kubu language any more, indicating that it was something to be ashamed of and clearly expecting all references to Kubu ways to be scoffed at as savage and primitive. They were astonished by Helmut's robust denials of this and his patent interest in and respect for all aspects of their traditional culture. For two hours he questioned them about the other clan deep in the interior whom they at first described as wild and dangerous. The 'wide feet' people who 'carry spears concealed behind their backs and stick them into strangers if they come too near'. However, when it came to discussing the numbers involved, they seemed remarkably well-informed saying that there were six hundred and seventy-eight more or less settled people ('narrow feet') near Markandang and another five hundred 'wide feet' under a very fierce chief called Alam Charaka deep in the forest near Kapas.

Gradually, Helmut persuaded them to reveal some Kubu words and he became quite excited when one or two sounded similar to the Mentawai equivalent. He began to note down a comparative vocabulary. I had understood that there were only a few small bands of Kubu left hiding in a vast area of swamp and jungle reaching to the foothills of the Darisan mountains far to the south-west. Now from these enquiries and others Helmut had made elsewhere, it appeared that there might be as many as three thousand semi-acculturated Kubu living on the fringes of the swamp and a further five thousand 'wild' ones in the interior. Other people I spoke to later put the figure higher still, saying that there were ten times this number, but since 'Kubu' has for long been the rudest thing one Sumatran can call another (closely followed by 'Batak'), these figures may have included other unrelated groups.

The most depressing fact to emerge during the evening concerned the wildlife of the region. This is the last stronghold of the rare Sumatran rhinoceros, the only Asian species with two horns, and the even rarer Javan rhinoceros is also known. Elephants, tigers, tapirs, wild dogs and civet cats as well as several varieties of large and exotic birds, including Argus and fire-back pheasants and the terrestrial Kuhau, an example of which we saw stuffed in the Bukittinggi museum, are also supposed to live there, but these Kubu told us that almost all the larger wildlife except monkeys and wild pig, had been virtually exterminated from the area they knew by the military using sophisticated weapons and travelling by jeep or by boat in the wet season. Whereas in Djambi, we had been warned to watch out for tigers, we now learned that these two families had never even heard of a tiger being seen locally for many years.

Helmut and I discussed the exciting potential for creating a really huge national park of perhaps one million hectares in what is probably the richest remaining wildlife region in all Indonesia. If there really were large numbers of nomadic Kubu still living there too, then Survival International should investigate the possibilities of playing a part as well, but there is so little information available on the whole area that further research is urgently needed. One of the main activities of the World Bank/Bonn University project, for which Helmut was working, was to investigate the viability of building a new road to run along the foothills of the mountains. It seemed at that stage that their conclusion was likely to be that it would be better to spend a much smaller sum improving the existing road system via Palembang to the east so that the isolated tribes and remaining colonies of wildlife in the critical, undisturbed, virgin country on the far side of the swamps, might be reprieved. But the threat would remain and I could once again imagine no man more capable of creating and administering such a park than Helmut.

We slept on the floor of the hut, our feet in the ashes of the small fire, and set off again before dawn, walking down to the river through a thick, wet mist. From here, we were to travel by canoe in an attempt to meet another group before cutting back to the road again by a different route. Denang and Amin took us in their two minute dugout canoes which leaked and threatened to overturn every moment as we threaded our way through the tangled undergrowth. The river twisted and turned back on itself, disappearing completely into the trees on either side whenever the rushes met in the middle so that we had to haul ourselves along by their stems. Still, even if progress was slow, I was glad of a chance to give my cut and blistered feet a rest before the long run back. Because we were travelling quietly on the open stretches of water, often hidden in patches of mist, we should have been in a good position to catch sight of animals drinking in the early morning light. Monkeys were plentiful in the treetops, shattering the stillness with their cries and crashes as they leapt; a herd of wild pigs rustled off leaving a muddy wallow and footprints on the bank; once I glimpsed a small deer raising its startled head from the water before flicking off into the shadows; but on the whole what the Kubu had said was borne out and we saw no traces of larger mammals.

The other Kubu we met were also disappointingly proud of their few pathetic civilized trappings and ashamed of their poverty, reminding me more of poor Brazilian settlers than proud, self-sufficient, jungle nomads. We returned, agreeing sadly that since this part of the swamp was likely to be exploited for oil production soon anyway, it might well be best to go the whole way and schedule it as one of the areas for a transmigration resettlement programme for the overcrowded island of Java. Indonesia's population is growing so fast that sheer pressure of numbers must soon push people into the wilder areas which only makes it all the more urgent to designate those areas which should receive protection before it is too late. One such certainly exists in southern Sumatra, beyond the point to which we penetrated, and perhaps the Indonesian government will demarcate a park there in time.

It has been a part of the evolutionary process since the world began for species of plants and animals to disappear through competition with more viable forms. This is a natural state of affairs and the way in which better adapted species have come into existence. It is often used as a reason for accepting the disappearance of alternative cultures and the 'civilizing' of hunter and gatherer societies which are unable to compete with a technologically superior dominant population. But these processes have in the past taken place over thousands, even hundreds of thousands or millions of years and one has only to look at some of the archaic forms of life still on earth and still playing their part in the diversity of the environment (such as sharks and opossums, which have changed little if at all for two hundred million years), while new and initially successful species have come and gone, to realize that a temporary advantage will not necessarily stand up to long-term realities. Moreover, through the very slowness of the process, the necessary diversity has been maintained to provide both a gene pool for future adaptations and the complex, rich and varied interaction of life forms vital to a stable ecology—that is the interrelationship and interdependence of organisms and their environment. What is happening now through man's efficient and rapid interference is all too often the wholesale elimination of alternatives and the creation of dangerous, inflexible conformity. Whereas in the past the disappearance of one variety, whether plant, insect or animal, was on balance replaced by other evolutionary developments, thereby increasing the diversity of life forms, the rate of change has, through man's agency, increased to alarming and dangerous proportions.

Whether by removing the necessary habitat or by physical destruction, we are reducing the options open to nature to achieve stability faster than we are learning how to impose a stability of our own making. Diversity is essential to sustaining life on earth and this applies to man no less than to other forms of life, for man is part of nature. All progress involves change, just as all construction involves destruction and few would suggest that the human race should not try to improve its position in relation to other species while at the same time striving to eliminate poverty, hunger and misery among its own members. However, this does not mean that we should attempt to impose a uniform life style upon all peoples, even those who actively reject it. This is especially true today when it is becoming increasingly apparent that the world does not possess sufficient natural resources to sustain a modern, materialist way of life for all the nearly four thousand million members of the human race.

Official government attitudes of countries having tribal minorities within their boundaries tend to show a remarkable unanimity in their desire to make the tribes conform to certain preconceived standards while at the same time asserting their right to be different. In Brazil, for all the provisions in the constitution protecting the Indians' lands and rights, efforts in recent years to 'integrate them into the national society' as rapidly as possible and to censure their 'backward' ways as representing a bar to progress are well documented. In Indonesia, the approach appears to be much the same. An article in the official publication *Indonesia* (No. 16, 1972) entitled 'The Isolated Ethnic Groups in Indonesia—tackling the problem of their development' by Achmadi, begins with a preamble condemning such terms as primitive, backward and uncivilized. It asserts that, 'Those people living in isolation also grow and develop like any other human being with their own thought, feelings and activity. They are normal people, and have a culture, although clearly this culture is not the same as that of more developed groups.

The term "non-cultured" is completely inaccurate; they are cultured, and, their culture is a result of adaptation to the prevailing situation and conditions.'

The article continues to define their case as a social problem which Indonesia 'whether it likes it or not, must tackle ... and create social justice' and also, significantly, as a national problem 'because it involves national and humanitarian prestige. The fact that there still are isolated and remote peoples, developing at too slow a pace, can affect a nation's prestige and the dignity of man in that country.' After enumerating the societies concerned, numbering some half million members excluding 'many, such as those in central Borneo and west Irian which have not been mentioned because they are still in the process of orientation, observation and registration', it concludes as follows: 'Operational designs for the development of isolated societies which are already in operation must be continually perfected both realistically and pragmatically, in order to fulfill our hope for the disappearance of isolated societies within the set time.' The 'set time' is, however, not given in the article.

While not questioning the good intentions of this government programme, although I find the belief that it is undignified for a country to tolerate the existence of ethnic minorities rather disturbing, I do feel that they have fallen into an all too familiar error in establishing their priorities. Those groups which, either through forced settlement on the edge of towns or the irredeemable loss of their lands through colonization, are suffering the hardships and problems of finding themselves regarded as second class citizens, certainly are a social problem and need every help to raise their status and standard of living to conform with that of their neighbours. The Kubu we saw fell into this category and, while the process is by no means as easy as it sounds on paper and indeed, through prejudice on the one hand and an inability to adapt rapidly on the other, may be virtually impossible, there seems to be no other course open for them. However, the other, still isolated, Kubu, living deeper in the interior and apparently still firm in their resolve to avoid permanent contact, should, for the time being at least, be left alone. It is their basic right and while closer contact with the outside world will inevitably develop there is no immediate urgency either for their own safety or in the interests of the nation that they should be settled, moved or otherwise interfered with. Rather their needs should be studied and a proper plan for their future evolved. This cannot come from preconceived notions of what is best for them, which would almost certainly result in the same disorientation, shock and shame suffered by their settled relations, but should instead arise from a careful and above all gradual assessment of their territorial, medical and social requirements. At the same time it is vital that they are given a fair chance to assess the nature of the society with which they must eventually establish a relationship. If their right to the land they occupy is assumed, the limits to it must also be defined and any rules which are imposed, such as the protection of certain species, the right of certain people to enter for whatever reason and the changes which are planned, must be explained to them and agreed with them so that they are aware of what is going on. This would clearly take a considerable time, during which the desire to change them would have to be resisted, requiring an unusual degree of restraint on the part of the authorities, but it is only in this way that their best interests could be secured. Meanwhile, the possibility of creating one of the largest and most exciting wildlife parks in south-east Asia could be examined, the boundaries demarcated and the necessary administration and research programme established

PART TWO

❧

Borneo

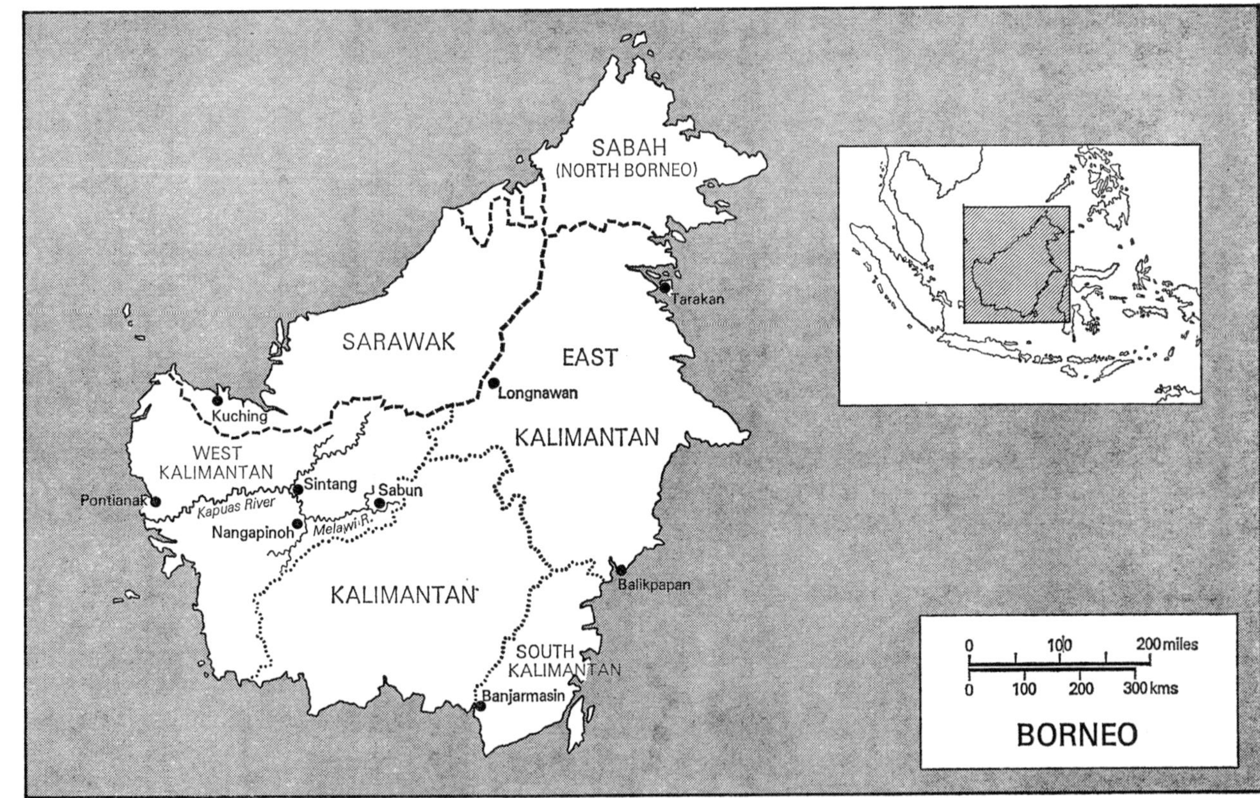
SABAH
(NORTH BORNEO)
SARAWAK
EAST
KALIMANTAN
Tarakan
Longnawan
Kuching
WEST
KALIMANTAN
Pontianak
Sintang
Sabun
Kapuas River
Nangapinoh
Melawi R.
KALIMANTAN
SOUTH
KALIMANTAN
Banjarmasin
Balikpapan
0
100
200 miles
0
100
200
300 kms
BORNEO

Kalimantan

❧

BORNEO is the third largest island in the world. By far the larger, and least known part, is Indonesian, while along the north-western coast lie Sarawak and Sabah (north Borneo) which belong to the Malaysia Federation with the tiny oil-rich sultanate of Brunei, a British protectorate, sandwiched between them. I had been to all of these in 1958, visiting the spectacular Niah caves where uncounted millions of bats and swiftlets roost by day and by night respectively, blackening the sky with aerial traffic jams at dawn and dusk, and where the remains of palaeolithic man, dating back from fifty to one hundred thousand years before Christ have been found. I had also stayed in Dayak longhouses on some of the rivers and been hospitably received by these once enthusiastic headhunters, who still kept clusters of dried skulls hanging in the rafters.

The name Dayak refers to all the indigenous proto-Malay and Malay peoples of the interior of Borneo, but they vary widely in culture and racial origins, representing successive waves of migration throughout history. Most used to live in longhouses, but recent administrations have made efforts to break up these communal dwellings where up to fifty or more families (we heard of one 'sixty-five door' longhouse) share one building. It seems to have been a feature of the Dutch administration of the outer islands as much as the present Indonesian one to feel that longhouses represented a barrier to progress. The motivation for either banning them and going as far as burning them down to punish the inhabitants or simply making continuing efforts to encourage the inhabitants to move to conventional villages usually arises from one of three preconceptions or a combination of all three. In the first place there is the puritanical belief that it is somehow immoral for families to live in such close association and that all sorts of licentious behaviour and disgusting orgies will take place if people are not separated by walls and space at night. Secondly it is assumed that the normal, healthy situation for man is the single family unit; that hygiene, social responsibility and work will suffer under communal living conditions. Finally, there is the often frankly admitted reason that such arrangements are harder to administer, police and keep a check of than regular rows of numbered houses near to a coast, road or river where numbers can be estimated at a glance and access to each family can be easily obtained. None of these reasons impress me as sufficiently valid to necessitate the social upheaval involved in implementing resettlement programmes but the process is still pursued with undiminished energy.

The Punan, on the other hand, shy forest nomads of the mountainous heart of the island, make only flimsy temporary shelters, but remarkably little is known about them and the term is often applied to anyone going on short forays into the jungle to hunt or collect jungle produce. Their numbers are thought to be very small now and they are not easy to locate, so that although I would have dearly liked to try and reach them—perhaps by flying to the old Dutch outpost of Longnawan near the centre of the island—it seemed more sensible to concentrate on a fairly remote Dayak group and spend some time with them instead. The colourful and culturally strong Ibans at the head waters of the Kapuas river looked, at first, like the best choice. Through their tradition of travelling widely and raiding around the coast of Sarawak, the Iban, although really riverine people, were known as sea Dayaks. Much of the energies of the three generations of Rajahs Brooke had been devoted to pacifying these ardent headhunters, but I gathered that living as they do now along the Sarawak/Kalimantan border, their spirit of independence was far from broken. However, due to continuing military activity against Communist guerillas in that region, there was little chance that we would be allowed to visit them.

Our only contact in Pontianak, the capital of western Kalimantan, was an introduction to the pilot of the light aeroplane which serviced the Protestant missions scattered about the territory. By chartering this, or fitting in with planned flights, we had hoped to reach an English anthropologist working with the Iban. However, we learned later that he had been summoned by the police to return to Jakarta to have his papers put in order. As luck would have it, he had flown out of Pontianak by the same 'plane on which we had arrived and we had somehow failed to bump into each other at the small but crowded airport. As a result, I had not been able to ask his advice about where to go during his absence.

The missionary pilot was flying the next day to Nangapinoh, the furthest inland Protestant post in western Kalimantan. It lay on the Melawi river, a southern tributary of the Kapuas, reaching up to the edge of central Kalimantan. For a small fortune, understandable in view of the high cost of maintaining aircraft in Borneo, we were able to hitch a lift. Flying across western Kalimantan I was surprised to see how little virgin forest there was left. The island is usually described as having most of its surface covered with dense, impenetrable vegetation. This was certainly not true of the land we now saw spread out below us for mile after mile. Almost all the level ground had been cleared and appeared abandoned, uninhabited and clothed in scrub. We only saw a few scattered areas under cultivation. It looked as though extensive slash-and-burn agriculture over a long period of time, and on poor soil, had created a situation similar to many parts of Brazil, where lush rain forest, supporting a rich and varied flora and fauna, had been converted into a barren waste for the sake of a few years' crops. Meanwhile other factors cause the population to increase, thereby accelerating the process and creating a difficult and often irreversible vicious circle. We passed some magnificent craggy limestone rocks rising up to a thousand metres, and on our return ten days later made a detour to the south over some more mountainous and heavily forested country. Even here the jungle was not as dense as I had expected and I could often see down to the ground between the trees. This indicated that the soil was weaker than in South America, where there is usually a blanket cover only broken by rivers. Two Indonesian timber prospectors, who flew with us on that occasion, became quite excited at the sight of these uncut acreages and indicated that their company would soon move in to exploit them. The largest single piece of woodland we saw, itself surrounded by burnt scrubland, could not have been more than fifty thousand hectares.

Removing these forests would be sure to change the whole ecology of the region and perhaps even the climate. Development planners see the question of timber extraction quite differently from social scientists and ecologists. Altering our environment has much wider implications than the short-term financial gains which accrue to an industry and, through taxation, to the host nation. When the industry is largely foreign based and uses imported labour, the need for the government concerned to examine the long-term effects of its presence and its operations is especially important. If an attempt is made to assess the social and cultural costs involved, the potential for development and the scope for secondary industries once the timber has been removed and the cost of rehabilitating and maintaining the resident population, it may well be found that, far from bringing benefits to the people, the eventual effect of the lumber business has been to lower their standard of living and remove their ability to be self-supporting.

Unfortunately, it is the voice of the extractive corporations which are at present heeded by the Indonesian government, although there is growing evidence, to judge from recent newspaper reports of student unrest in Jakarta during the Japanese prime minister's visit, that this section of the community at least is aware of the dangers of too much dependence on foreign capital.

Nangapinoh, at the junction of the Melawi and Pinoh rivers, was a pretty sight from the air; a town built completely of wood with several rows of barges-cum-houseboats moored along the bank. The airstrip, a short stretch of grass running over the dome of a little hill, lay some distance from the river. John van Patten, the resident American missionary, had kindly come out to meet us in his mini tractor and trailer, the only vehicle in town, in which he drove us to the office of the *camat* (prefect). A radio message through the missionary network had alerted the military and civil authorities to our arrival, indicating that we were tourists. The *camat* gave us a most friendly welcome, placing all his resources at our disposal and inviting us to stay in the prefecture where a room had been prepared for us with mattresses on the floor. We explained that we hoped to hire a boat and ascend the Melawi river as far as possible in the time available, visiting and staying in Dayak longhouses along the way. The *camat* summoned a young local man working in his office. He was smartly dressed in a khaki uniform and spoke a few words of English. It was explained to us that he had been appointed for the duration of our stay as our guide and escort since he had been born far up the Melawi river to a Dayak father and Chinese mother and so had friends and relations all over the place. At first we were a little doubtful as to how much of an asset this would be, remembering in particular an official guide we had had in Brazil who had often made our lives a misery there. Amri Bachtiar, however, was quite different and proved to be an excellent travelling companion; understanding of and sympathetic with our particular interest in *adat* and Dayak life, while at the same time taking great pains to make the journey as comfortable as possible. It was a great relief to have with us someone who, whenever we stopped at a long-house, would go ahead explaining who we were and what we wanted; someone who saw that food was provided, either from the few stores we took with us or more usually by the people with whom we stayed. On the rare occasions when we were allowed to pay for anything he made sure we paid a fair and reasonable price and he did all this with great verve and enthusiasm, never throwing his weight around with his country cousins but cheerfully greeting old friends and making new ones so that we always felt welcomed and at home.

Much of the night we spent in Nangapinoh was devoted to striking a bargain with the owner of the only operational outboard motor there. Without this, travel up river would have been impossibly slow so that he had me over a barrel and knew it. However we finally agreed a price of thirty pounds to include a boat and two boatmen for a week which was not unreasonable, and by half past eight the next morning we were able to set off. Walking through the town to shop for some food to take with us we were escorted by a crowd of about one hundred and fifty small children who chanted English words they had learnt at school. They were friendly and excited by our presence, but occasionally the feeling of being a glorified Pied Piper, stared at so intensely and from such close range that every action was a cause for comment and giggles, became too much for me. When this happened I would turn and roar at them like a lion causing a delighted stampede for shelter, during which one of the smallest usually fell and was trampled on needing comfort and reassurance that we were not *really* dangerous. The main street of Nangapinoh is lined with rather fine wooden colonial houses on stilts. A raised wooden sidewalk, bordered with little Chinese stores, means that one can walk its length dry shod avoiding the mud and puddles in between. A fair proportion of the population live on the houseboats, taking off occasionally to spend weeks slowly chugging down the stream to Pontianak and trading along the river bank.

Although the Melawi was in spate, carrying a lot of flotsam and sometimes whole trees, our boat, with its twenty horsepower motor, made excellent speed against the fast current. For the first day or two we could see that beyond the fringe of trees on the river's edge, much of the land had been burnt and cleared at some time and was now covered in scrub. Bare hills, coated in coarse grass, were visible in the distance and it was not until we had passed the first rapids and reached higher and less navigable reaches of the river that the forest stretched away over mountain and valley alike. Most of the cultivated land and savannah in Kalimantan is at present in the west and we were seeing the result of a long period of indigenous farming combined with timber extraction from the coast. But today a large majority of the lumber companies clearing the jungle are working in the east and south of the island so that soon the situation will be similar there too.

In the evening we reached a Chinese trader's house where we stopped and were fed on mouse deer and rice. Most of the Chinese have been forced to move from the rivers of western Kalimantan to settlements around Pontianak where life is not easy for them as they are said to be cheated and abused, their possessions confiscated and their liberty threatened. We, ourselves, had seen a frail old Chinese lady surrounded by a crowd of shouting youths, who had jostled and teased her while she defended herself with her umbrella. All this has come about since the 1965 coup when many Chinese were massacred as suspected Communists. Guerilla activity in the north, as well as jealousy for their past financial dominance, continues to make their lives difficult. Our trader, by contrast, seemed to be fairly prosperous, although he said that there were not many of his people left so far inland. His main business was in nuts for making into palm oil which, he told us, were exported to Germany and Japan, as well as some wild rubber brought to him by the Dayaks. In exchange he traded plastic buckets, soap, torch batteries and cloth.

It was suggested that we might like to sleep there, but I explained that if possible I would prefer to go to a longhouse if there was one not too far away. Amri now showed his mettle, galvanizing our two silent boatmen, Ahin and Among, into action. They looked surprised at the idea of setting out again after dark and I had the impression that on my own it would not have been so easy to shift them. Amri said he knew of a longhouse at Tanjung Bringin hidden away up a side river nearby which we would find most interesting as the people had been headhunters only twenty years before and they were great dancers and musicians. For nearly an hour we groped our way dangerously fast through the blackness of a mysterious twisting stream with the trees almost meeting overhead and weird skeletons of dead branches rearing up out of the water. Among stood in the front with my torch picking out the snags and guiding us around bends. A fierce thunderstorm was raging a few miles away and every few minutes the whole scene was illuminated by a flash of lightning.

When we finally spotted a light from the bank Amri jumped ashore and disappeared to announce our arrival. He returned glum and disappointed, explaining to me in a whisper that the group had been completely 'ruined' since he was last there, as the Protestant missionary had reached them, shown them how to build a modern house and 'completely changed their ways'. Since Amri and I had not discussed the tricky problem of missionary activity among isolated peoples, and he had no knowledge of my views on the matter—except that I was not, myself, a missionary—I found his attitude interesting and rather encouraging. He was, himself, a Muslim so naturally critical of Christian missions. He was also eager to please us by taking us to Dayak communities, which were as interesting and 'original' as possible. At the same time I had assumed that with his relatively sophisticated urban background, and the prestige of his uniform and official status, he would tend to look down on tribal life, regarding it at least with tolerant condescension. Instead I was beginning to learn, to my surprise, that his mind was very open and that his own evident ambition to succeed as a civil servant was tempered with a genuine respect for Dayaks and their traditions. This was one of the most encouraging and admirable features of many of the Indonesians we met throughout the country. Whereas in South America we had grown used to meeting a consistent disapprobation by petty officials of the native tribes with their 'dirty habits' and inferior life style, we were to find in Indonesia that far more of those in positions of authority genuinely appeared not to regard the isolated tribes as inferior, although at the same time they seldom went so far as to question the benefits which instant civilization would bring them.

The headman of the village took us to his house and showed us where we could sleep. Men, women and children with light skins, brown wavy hair and dark eyes, crowded in to see us and to ask us questions. Since they had so recently been converted by a fundamentalist Protestant they were most interested in finding out about our own brand of religion. This was to be a subject which dogged us throughout our time in Indonesia. How does one explain in simple terms, and with limited language, the respective dogmas of Roman Catholicism and the various brands of Protestantism? In particular, we had to try and identify Anglican attitudes. My personal view has always been that the Church of England lies much closer to the Church of Rome than to the extreme Protestant beliefs held by the American missions, so active in many of the more remote parts of the world. Marika produced a wildly oversimplified formula which we found ideal in identifying our position when in a situation where what we saw as the two extreme wings of Christian belief confronted each other in vying for a tribe's allegiance. She would take a piece of paper and on it write Roman Catholic and Protestant in the top two corners. Drawing lines from each to the centre of the sheet she would put Church of England there, indicating that this was the sect to which we belonged. This ecumenical solution had the advantage of implying, albeit rather dishonestly, that in our country we had overcome the problem of marrying the divergent outlooks of the two faiths, while at the same time freeing us from having to identify too closely with whichever was dominant in the particular house or village in which we were staying.

The most noticeable change wrought at Tanjung Bringin was that the entire community had been dissuaded from smoking. Since cigarettes were far and away the most valuable commodity in every other place we visited throughout Indonesia, and all generations smoked like chimneys when not chewing betel, this was no small achievement. We asked if it was all right for us to smoke and were assured that this was perfectly acceptable, although the pained looks of craving from some of the old men made me feel guilty. I spotted Marika subverting all the missionaries' efforts by slipping a packet to one or two, who then furtively made their way outside into the darkness.

Just as we were about to go to bed, tired after the long day in the burning sun on the river, gongs sounded in the distance and we were invited to go to the longhouse where Amri said the people were going to dance. We climbed down the steps from the headman's 'modern' single family house to find that the rest of the village consisted of one twenty-door longhouse, set further back from the river bank. The great gallery was crowded with people, their faces illuminated by a few oil lamps which threw shadows into the dark corners of the rafters where paddles, fishtraps and pots were stored. Five men, stripped to the waist, sat in the centre playing on gongs and filling the air with a loud bouncy rhythm. There was a lot of discussion about who was going to dance and at last four boys, wearing white singlets, were prevailed upon to take the floor. Giggling and stumbling they thumped inelegantly about, nudging each other and hamming it up. One of the old men became angry and shouted at them to do it properly. At this they stopped and went off looking sullen and muttering. The atmosphere became tense and embarrassing, but before I could suggest that it really didn't matter Amri leapt to his feet and encouraged others to try, demonstrating in an extrovert and endearing way steps he remembered from his childhood. Some women, dressed in colourful embroidered shirts and long sarongs, swayed together from side to side to a slow rhythm, their eyes closed in a clear effort to capture the mood and spirit of half-forgotten trances. Others took their places and gradually the tempo quickened and the standard of dancing improved. Then, unexpectedly and with much clapping and laughter, a short dark boy of about sixteen was pushed forward. He, too, wore a singlet, but it had a vivid butterfly painted on it, and the moment he began to dance his intensity and concentration stilled the chatter and the giggles from the background. Wheeling and dipping, like a bird in flight, he leaped and twisted over the uneven floor, fluttering his arms and bending to touch the ground. At the end he stood silent, with head bowed. Then, taking an old brass-handled sword—the ceremonial weapon of that longhouse—and to a faster and more stirring beat, he danced the story of a legendary battle, slashing about him with controlled grace and leaping high into the air as the blade glinted in the dim light, and his body glistened with sweat. We were told that he had only recently arrived from a distant longhouse, far in the interior, to attend the school set up by the mission.

Seeing how impressed we were by this performance, others now tried their hand but none were in the same league as the 'butterfly boy'. We found it sad that whereas at first they had been embarrassed to dance at all, thinking that we would laugh at them and presumably having been told by the missionary that such things were decadent and primitive, they were now embarrassed at their inability to do it properly, and their awkwardness and lack of grace.

Returning at first light to the main river, we headed upstream again passing few settlements before Manukung, where the *camat*, an intelligent, educated man called

Shabaruddin Yahya, gave us lunch. He told us that there were seventeen thousand people in his district living in seventy-seven villages. Apart from the coastal Malays, who had settled in the area, there were four Dayak groups under his control. These were the Limbai to whom the people of Tanjung Bringin belonged; the Kenyilu; the Ransa and the Kubin. We talked about the problems facing the region in the future. For two years the rice crops had been poor due to the failure of the rains, and he told us that a situation close to famine was approaching. With rice reaching two hundred rupiahs (about twenty pence) per kilo, even more than it costs in Jakarta, and with little opportunity for the people to earn the money to buy it, it seemed that matters could only become worse. The rivers are hard to fish for most of the year as nets are carried away by the fast current, or destroyed by the logs floating downstream. Little success has been had with efforts to introduce new crops and so reduce the dependence on rice. As the population increases along the river bank, and the forest is reduced by slash-and-burn agriculture and the development of timber concessions, land becomes exhausted. Although the *camat* was energetic and anxious to improve the people's lot, I found it hard to see what the future might hold. The assumption that introducing western culture in all its forms, from single houses in preference to longhouses, to modern clothes, outboard motors, schools, utensils and attitudes, would in some way make people's lives better, seemed to me to be based on a false premise. All these things may, and probably will, come to the Dayaks in time, but without a secure and economic basis they are more likely to cause suffering and discontent. A far more urgent priority should be to see where the existing lifestyle falls short of satisfying needs and attempt to find ways of improving it. This would surely be much better than compounding the problem by encouraging change for its own sake and thereby introducing needs which cannot be satisfied.

These thoughts were reinforced when we met the young

Dutch Roman Catholic priest at our next stop, Serawai. His house and school was on a hill behind the town, where a row of shops faced the water. We walked there through the rain which had fallen for most of that day so that we had travelled on the river, huddled under our invaluable plastic sheet. He had been there for four and a half years, and told us that we were the first Europeans to call on him for two years since a team of Frenchmen, prospecting for uranium, had arrived. As far as he knew, no Europeans had gone much further up the Melawi in the direction in which we were headed, although the Indonesian authorities had some outposts there. In his opinion, the reason for the general hunger of the Dayaks was that they were able to grow only one crop of rice a year, and so laid themselves open to disaster when it failed. He had tried to show them how to guard against this, bringing beans, tomatoes and other seeds in, and demonstrating how to plant them and care for them, but he had become disillusioned by the Dayak's unwillingness to learn new techniques and their lack of a desire to change. 'These people', he said, 'don't seem able to change—they neither want to nor can.'

He was more enthusiastic about the opportunities for hunting game, saying that the jungle was rich in deer and wild pigs. A few of the locals had rifles, but mostly they used spears often leaving them in spring traps. These resulted in frequent severe injuries with which he had to deal when people walked into the trip wire and received a spear through the groin or thigh. What with his medical work and trying to provide education for all the children in the district, there was little or no time left for other matters. He believed that there was no reason why ways should not be found to avoid disaster befalling the Melawi river, but that it would require expert study and research into agricultural techniques which were not likely to be forthcoming in the near future. He clearly thought us quite mad when we bade leave of him and set off once more in a torrential downpour, rather than wait for the weather to improve. We explained regretfully that time was too short for such luxuries, but, speaking to one who had been stuck in the same place for over four years, we realized that we had different concepts of time.

The two longhouses at Tontang, which we reached about evening, stood on the river bank behind a row of palm trees. We swam from a raft on the shore, diving into the deep, warm, muddy water and washing ourselves and our clothes. There was a much better atmosphere here with laughter and friendliness and round-eyed groups of little children creeping closer and staring at us with rapt interest as we sat on exquisitely woven rattan mats and were fed on rice and hot spicy morsels of meat. The cigarettes and slabs of tobacco we had brought as presents were much appreciated, and musical instruments were brought out and played without Amri having to prompt anyone. The most impressive was a set of five pipes attached to a gourd with a spout on which the player sucked, producing a pleasant mellow sound. The longest pipe measured over four feet and the others between two and three. It was called a *kerone*, and intricate tunes were played on it by stopping holes in the pipes with the fingers. There were also two-stringed guitars, with solid wooden sound boxes, called *kenyapi*, a six-stringed guitar called *gambús*, drums, and a row of little high pitched gongs mounted on a log. All these were played in turn, and together, making a fair amount of reasonably harmonious noise so that dancing also began spontaneously. Most of the men wore shirts and trousers, but the first to dance, incongruously, put on a loin cloth over his trousers; also a turban on his head. Little girls danced hand in hand around a sort of maypole, festooned with coloured rags, and another man went and changed into women's clothes. He danced a woman's dance, with a headscarf covering his face as he waggled his hips and put on a really quite sophisticated transvestite act which made everyone laugh. Strong rice wine, also I imagine forbidden to converts, was passed round freely and tasted delicious.

At about midnight we went outside for a walk in the bright moonlight. In between the palm trees were several carved wooden figures on poles looking strange and sinister in silhouette. The largest, about five metres long, lay on its side like an Easter Island statue; while others were only the size of children. Some had bald heads with comic smiling faces, and there was one very serious gentleman in a suit with his hands at his side and a little black cap on his head. We walked some way along the bank, disturbing an occasional pig asleep in the long grass, and looking down on the big shiny river flooding past; still over seventy metres wide, although over three hundred kilometres from the coast. At the end of the village a stream ran into the main river through a narrow cutting spanned by a well-made bridge, with bright yellow railings. It seemed so smart and out of place in the jungle that we felt, for a moment, that we might have been in Hyde Park looking out over the Serpentine, but that may just have been due to the rice wine.

At Ambalou we called on the last *camat* on the Melawi river. After the best part of a day spent on the gradually narrowing river, with the hills drawing closer on both sides and the jungle becoming more wild and beautiful; after seeing only an occasional canoe and very few signs of human habitation for mile after mile, it was something of a shock to walk into the Kafkaesque atmosphere of the *camat*'s office. In a modern concrete house, under a corrugated iron roof, three uniformed clerks sat at metal tables, clattering away busily on typewriters. Reams of paper were stacked around the walls, and a vast map was covered with different coloured pins. This office controlled the whole of the little known region stretching up to the borders of central Kalimantan. The Dayaks from here on, we were told, were mostly Ot Danum, with some Mentebah, Muhakan and Melahuh Nyangai. There were also said to be Punan around, but 'we don't see *them*'. The *camat*, in his immaculate military uniform and stuck in one of the remotest Indonesian outposts with no airstrip or outboard motor, and several weeks away from Pontianak by river barge, naturally longed for development to take place soon. He proudly showed us areas of virgin forest on the map, which had been scheduled for timber concessions, saying that some large foreign companies had expressed interest and would, he hoped, soon move into the area.

On my return to England I learnt how near his hopes are to being realized, and this has already raised grave fears in scientific circles as to the long-term effects of such development. By 1970 one hundred and sixty-eight timbering concessions had been granted in Kalimantan, and this number must have greatly increased in the last three years. Nearly all have gone to foreign corporations, the largest being American owned, and the others being Japanese, Philippino, French, Korean, Hong Kong and Malaysian. In eastern Kalimantan alone, where most of the work to date has been undertaken, foreign concession holders were actively engaged in logging operations covering a total concession area of 5·7 million hectares by June 1972. The danger of operations on this scale, in areas which have not been properly studied, is that the indigenous plant life and local knowledge of its value and potential will be destroyed and lost. This is indispensable to the future agriculture and economy of the region once the forest cover is removed. Timber operations rapidly disturb the ecosystem, threaten many species of wild life with extinction and dislocate the indigenous population before plans can be made for their future. Proper estimates of a people's needs, and the effects of rapid change upon them, cannot be made without their cultures and way of life being studied. Very few anthropologists have worked in Kalimantan, and what has been recorded about the cultures has seldom taken into account considerations of the future.

As elsewhere, research has tended to concentrate on recording the customs and social structures of the Dayaks. Further study of their relationship with their environment, their needs and the effects which change will have upon them would clearly be of inestimable value in assessing the correct course which development and the extraction of natural resources should take. The Food and Agricultural Organization of the United Nations recognizes these dangers and the tremendous need to create gene banks of varied food sources for potential use in differing regions. An emergency survey has been set up. But little else is being done in this field, and at the present rate time will soon run out and the information will have been lost. With the threat of massive world food shortages growing closer every year it is as astonishing that vast areas, such as Kalimantan, should be allowed to become barren wastelands, as it is that alternative sources of food should be allowed to be destroyed in the short-term exploitation of timber.

All this takes no account of the rights of the indigenous inhabitants of these areas. As we have seen, they are at present only barely able to scratch a living from the relatively densely populated river banks, and have to supplement their agriculture by hunting in the forests. Remove these and they will starve; and yet the forests themselves are demonstrably productive; trees, plants and wildlife abound. How much more significant it would be for the wellbeing of mankind if as much effort were put into finding ways of harnessing that potential, as is currently being expended in cutting it all down.

I did not attempt to express my misgivings to the *camat* of Ambalou, but instead thanked him for his help and courtesy, had a good look at his excellent map which showed how inaccurate all others I had seen of the area were, and then continued the journey. We turned up the Ambalou river itself, as this was nearly as large as the main river and said to be navigable for a longer distance. Soon there were shallows and rapids through which our little boat bucked and plunged, with spray breaking over us. The banks came closer together, and large trees with orchids in them overhung the river, trailing lianas into the water. The highest point we reached was the village of Sabun, above which the river cascaded through a gap between high boulders, foaming and crashing with white spray. We swam below the waterfall, off a wide, black, slippery rock, across which Marika, having lost her footing, bounced like a rubber ball before disappearing beneath the surface. Luckily, she was wet already by this time as it was raining again so, apart from the bruises, no harm was done. Back in the longhouse we hung up all our clothes to dry. Several of the women in Sabun were wearing enormous, brightly patterned coolie hats over a metre across, finely woven from rattan and decorated at the crown with assorted charms and pieces of cloth. In the very centre of each was a tuft of black human hair, like a plume on a helmet. Marika wanted to try and persuade one of the ladies to sell her one of these hats, but in the end we decided that it would never survive the rest of the journey and so we bought a sleeping mat instead. It had been laid out for us as honoured guests, the first Europeans in Sabun, they said, and we had admired the fine intricate coloured patterns of the rattan weave. Trying to strike a balance between haggling too hard and using our authority and position to beat the price down, while at the same time not accepting the asking price and paying an exorbitant sum, was not easy, but they solemnly assured us that such a mat took a year to make, and they were such gentle friendly people, that we eventually paid about four pounds which Amri said was fair and more or less double what anyone else would pay. They also had very fine chickens at Sabun; forty or fifty of them perched at night in a tree beside the longhouse guarded by healthy hunting dogs, fat by Indonesian standards, which slept under the house. Most of the hens were white or speckled, but the cocks were multicoloured jungle fowl with a proud carriage like fighting cocks and long streaming tails.

There was much talk at Sabun of a gigantic waterfall, supposedly the biggest in Kalimantan, not far away. We would have very much liked to try and reach it, since it was

Batak village on Samosir Island, Lake Toba. Traditional houses are now being re-roofed with corrugated iron.

Large communal Karo Batak houses near Kabanjahe. Eight families live in each house, sharing four communal fires.

Mentawaian family on Siberut. The men prefer bark to cotton for loin cloths and the woman's skirt is made of palm leaves.

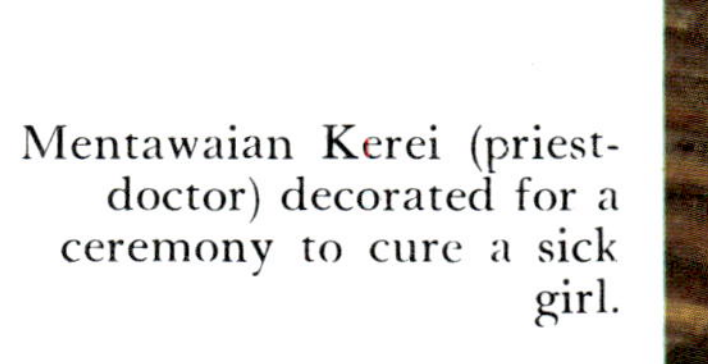

Mentawaian Kerei (priest-doctor) decorated for a ceremony to cure a sick girl.

The Kerei strokes a pig to calm it and placate its spirit before slaughter.

Mentawaian boy with wooden plaque commemorating a dead relation.

The Sakaliou *uma.*

The Mentawaians have n
rifles but hunt entirely wit
bows and arrow

Mud road made by Philippino lumber camp on Siberut.

Mentawaian family on one of the large inland rivers on Siberut.

Gongs and drums bei
played at night in a Day
long house on a tributa
of the Melawi riv

The five-piped wi
instrument (*kerone*) and
two-string guitar (*kenyap*
being played in a Day
long hou

The fish market at Palembang, Sumatra.

Ritual carved effigies outside the long house at Sabun.

Manhandling the dugout through rapids on the Ambalau river.

Bugis proa moored off the beach at Bira in southern Sulawesi.

Wet rice fields (*Sawah*) in Toraja country.

Palawa, Toraja village.

Toraja house.

Carved wooden figures on a cliff ledge outside Toraja funeral caves.

Male relations, servants and friends, dancing around the bier at a Toraja funeral.

Toraja rock graves at Lokomata.

In the heart of Tana Towa where no European had been allowed before.

A man of Tana Towa.

Hua Ulu village.

Hua Ulu house with carving on the uprights.

Hua Ulu man making fire with flint and tinder.

Dani village in the Baliem Valley.

Dani women pounding banana stems at the salt spring.

The fifty-year-old mummy at Aikima village.

Dani woman and child in the Baliem Valley.

Playing on a mouth harp.

Dani warrior at Yiweka wearing a headdress made of cus-cus and bird of paradise feathers, cowrie shells and koteka.

Asmat warriors with spears at Agats.

said that no outsider had ever seen it, nor, indeed, did it seem to have been even flown over. However, time was too short and we had to abandon the idea. According to the *camat* of Ambalou it was somewhere up the Jengonoi river and would take about two and a half days to reach from Sabun by canoe and on foot, but none of his staff had ever been there. There were also said to be some groups of Punan living near to it, which only made having to turn back all the more frustrating.

On our way down the river again the sun often shone so that it became unbearably hot and our new mat came in useful as a shelter. Once more we stayed in different longhouses and grew used to the easy communal life. It seemed to me that the Dayaks had solved one of the problems which beset our society, albeit from different motives. They probably began living under one roof for reasons of security, while we build tower blocks because of the shortage of land in urban areas. But where our blocks of flats are often lonely soulless places, with impersonal playgrounds far from parental observation and lacking contact between neighbours, the longhouse provides the best of both worlds. Each family has its own front door and private quarters with storerooms, sleeping accommodation and a kitchen at the back. The remaining half of the building, with a long gallery running its entire length, fulfils the function of the so often sadly missed back street where children can play in safety; women can sit together and gossip as they work; men can meet and talk and plan the hunt, to say nothing of dancing, drinking and flirting of an evening. It would not be too difficult to adapt the concept for modern housing development stacking, as it were, one longhouse upon another. The galleries might be glass fronted, providing light and a view, perhaps with terraces sticking out where tiny gardens could be planted. Individual front doors and a sense of community should overcome the problem of vandalism, and the elderly, once more, could have a rôle in life, sitting outside and watching their grandchildren while they chatted to their neighbours. There might even be a shop or two providing different services on each floor. It is probably too idealistic a solution for our problems of urban overcrowding, but it works for the Dayaks and I can see no good reason why it should not be satisfactorily adapted for our society.

Strangely enough it is an attitude implicit in many of Corbusier's plans for communal 'freehold maisonettes' as illustrated in his book *Towards a New Architecture* written in 1923. In it he questions the growing obsession with wasteful detached houses, realizing that these will not be possible for all in crowded areas while at the same time forecasting the need for the family to become part of a greater social unit and escape from a 'snail shell' mentality. It is sad that subsequent urban development has so often failed to take into account the wider social implications with which he was as much concerned as the architecture.

In spite of the obvious poverty we were always given enough to eat in the longhouses. This impression of poverty among the Dayaks of the Melawi river seemed to me to arise from two quite separate causes. In the first place there was a clear shortage of food and the other necessities of life. But as important as this to the people was the awareness of a lack of trappings of a materialist society which had been brought home to them by contact over a long period with the coastal settlers and by an inability to afford the trade goods offered by the Chinese barge owners.

However there would always be a large communal bowl of steaming boiled rice, into which we all dipped, rolling the rice into a ball before popping it into our mouths. Usually there were one or two small dishes of fish, chicken or deer, and a special saucer of very hot spice which I tended to avoid, although Marika's ability to consume the fieriest concoctions never failed to impress. Lots of hot sweet tea in thimble-sized glasses before and after—we had bought packets of tea and sugar in Nangapinoh as presents—but we very seldom had any fruit. There was one excellent fleshy nut, rather like a lychee with a stone in it, called a *buah kelenking*, which we had occasionally, but no bananas, for example, which I felt efforts could well be made to introduce. The desire for, and lack of, sweet things was proved by the ecstasy with which the children eagerly accepted sweets from the packets we had brought with us, rushing off to show them to their parents and religiously sharing them out.

We grew used to having our every action observed with rapt attention—only the very young and the very old were blasé about our presence—and were constantly impressed by the beautiful manners of young and old alike. We almost never heard a child cry and noticed that even the teenage boys were not ashamed to nurse and care for the smallest babies. We saw some sickness and felt the usual sense of frustration at not being qualified to help. In particular, I remember one pathetically weak baby boy with ice cold hands and feet and a pulse rate of one hundred and forty. Suspecting that he was suffering from malaria, we prescribed a quarter of a paludrin and half an aspirin, leaving a supply with his parents, but it seemed unlikely that he would live without hospital treatment and that, we had to accept, was quite impossible. The shortage of doctors in the outlying areas of Indonesia is acute and where those who have qualified can earn more working in the towns it is hardly surprising that few are prepared to endure the discomfort and deprivation of long journeys into the interior. When the population is widely scattered and too poor either to travel to the coast or pay for treatment on arrival, there is no alternative to relying on the traditional methods by which they have survived in the past. The danger lies in discrediting these to such an extent that a vacuum is created causing misery and hopelessness.

Back in Nangapinoh Amri excused himself as soon as we landed, saying that his wife had been due to have a baby while we were away. He returned later to tell us that she had had a son, whom he wanted to call Tenison Amri

Bachtiar if I would give my permission. Highly flattered, I gave him my compass as a christening present and promised to send him a card on his birthday, the following 1st April.

The missionary pilot, who flew us back to Pontianak, felt that the Dayaks in general needed a good 'kick in the backside to get them moving again'. He was surprisingly outspoken and ready to put forward fresh ideas about what they needed if they were to become strong and effective again.

'These people are at a very low ebb just now. They have lost all confidence in themselves through being exploited, enslaved and told that they are stupid, lazy and inferior for so long, so that now they have come to believe it themselves.' Like several others I spoke to, he believed that a change to wet rice cultivation represented the Dayaks' best hope of growing enough food to be self-supporting. 'The trouble is this means a lot more hard work in the first year because they have to dig ditches and banks so as to make the paddies. If they would only do this, they could go on growing rice on the same land year after year and not have to clear new land all the time, but when we suggest it they always give the excuse, "We're too lazy to do that sort of thing". I really wish a mean, tough Dayak would come along and give these people a lead—show them that they can make their own way in the world.' He had worked for a time in New Guinea, flying to the Baliem valley, and admired the tough tribesmen he had met there, 'Those Dani walk around naked except for their penis gourds, but they wear them with style and look a lot better than the Dayaks in their miserable rags! The Dayaks must have been proud and self-confident once; I'd like to see them become like that again.'

Strong words for a Protestant missionary, and ones I felt fully in agreement with, but I also knew that we would never see eye to eye on the methods since a prerequisite of such pride must be a secure cultural base, which the very process of conversion to strict fundamentalist Christianity, with all its new rules and prohibitions, can only undermine.

The man I most wanted to see in Kalimantan was Victor King, the young British anthropologist, who had been working with the Iban on the Sarawak border. He was back in Pontianak, having had his papers renewed in Jakarta, and we were able to spend an evening together. Only a handful of anthropologists have worked in western Kalimantan and it was invaluable to be able to talk to someone who knew his subject, and had read all the available literature. His own view was gloomy. While he had seen no indications of real oppression through forced change, he felt sure that the culture was slowly dying. Many of the Dayak groups had been exploited for centuries as a source of slaves by the Arab Sultanates which reduced their numbers and caused them to fragment and flee into the interior. Then, later, the Chinese had taken over the control of all commerce and trade, so that when they were mostly removed in recent years, a vacuum was left behind which neither the Dayaks nor the coastal Malays were capable of filling, and, as a result, the people go hungry. Meanwhile, western influences creep in, creating needs which cannot be satisfied and causing discontent and misery. The Iban were a much tougher, prouder people who had always been great travellers. They were able to trade across the border and down to Kuching which helped them to sustain a more prosperous economy. However, their very success was a danger to them as the Indonesian authorities were suspicious of their travels and tended to regard their very strength and independence as a threat to national security. In a way he felt that people like the Kantu, who had been so brow-beaten over the years into believing that they were inferior, had an easier time of it, responding more readily to change of any sort. From photographs he showed me, it was evident that the Iban have a more colourful and viable culture than the peoples we had been with on the Melawi river, as well as wearing much more exotic traditional clothes. On the other hand, he had seen very few musical instruments such as we described, and had found the Iban much less prone to dancing.

He had come across no Punan and believed that most of them are now settled, although if they really are as shy and retiring as people say, it is not impossible that quite large groups may still be hiding deep in the interior. Wild life he had seen included deer, civet cats, wild pig and crocodiles. Orang-utan were, he said, quite regularly sold in the markets, which is, of course, illegal, as well as bad. The rare rhinoceros was, he thought, quite probably extinct.

We agreed that the first priority was a lot more research into both the peoples and their problems. The most immediate outcome of this should be increased medical aid and perhaps a birth control programme, which would not be difficult to provide using the existing networks of rivers for communications. Secondly, intense research into agricultural techniques should be undertaken, both as regards the existing rice cultivation and also by examining the possibilities of developing alternative indigenous sources of food. Only when the local economy was on a firmer footing, and some semblance of independence and security had been established, should roads, lumber camps and mineral exploitation, with all their attendant effects upon the local population, be introduced. At present these priorities appear to be being applied in reverse order and this can only have a catastrophic effect on the indigenous communities. As roads penetrate their territory, their forests are cut down and their land either taken from them or turned into scrub, they will have no alternative but to drift to the coast where they will become a disorientated and discontented shanty town problem. Meanwhile, the rich interior will have been raped of its timber, causing the sterilization of all its other potential. It is most unlikely that the forests will grow again of their own accord, and there is no indication that replanting is part of the plans of any of the timber concessionaires. According to the *Bulletin of Indonesian Economic Studies* (8, 128): 'For tropical rain forests, research and practical experience in Malaysia and elsewhere indicate that the assumption of natural regeneration in forests is dubious to say the least.' Timber is Indonesia's third biggest export and about three quarters of current production comes from Kalimantan. I left Pontianak feeling that unless there was to be a major shift in government policy towards the sale of timber concessions to foreign and multi-national companies, the future for the Dayaks is likely to be bleak indeed.

PART THREE

❧

Celebes (Sulawesi)

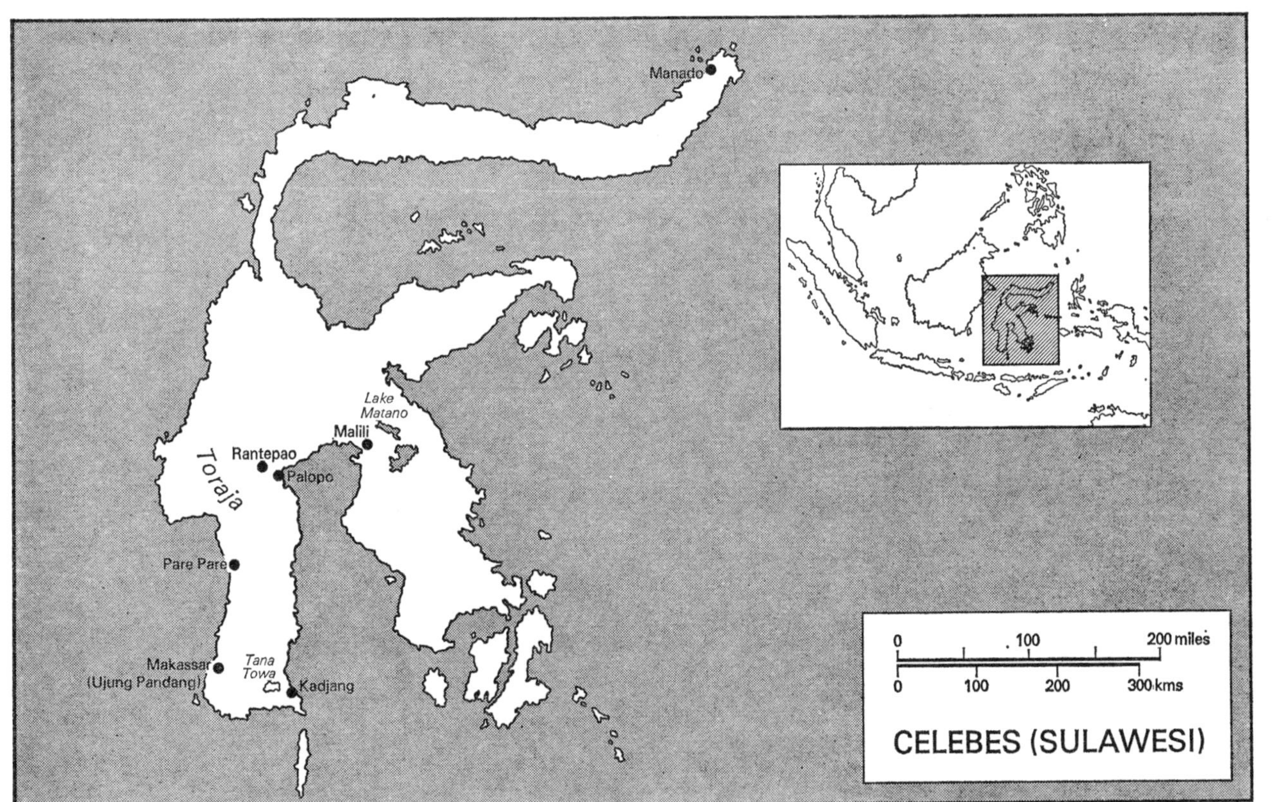
Manado
Lake
Matano
Malili
Rantepao
Palopo
Toraja
Pare Pare
Makassar
(Ujung Pandang)
Tana
Towa
Kadjang
0
100
200 miles
0
100
200
300 kms
CELEBES (SULAWESI)

Toraja

❧

To the east of Borneo lies the curiously shaped island of Celebes; its four mountainous arms curve away between three hundred and six hundred kilometres each, one to the north, one to the south and two to the east. Near the centre, at the root of the southern arm, live the Toraja—a tough, warlike people with a culture somewhat similar to the Bataks, and with possibly similar origins. Headhunters and animists, they held out in their mountain strongholds against all attacks from the coastal peoples until finally conquered and pacified by the Dutch in 1907. Since then, with the introduction of wet rice cultivation, they have become successful, energetic farmers and, in spite of considerable missionary activity, still largely practise their traditional customs and rituals, and continue to build, and live in, even more dramatically roofed and highly decorated houses than the Toba Bataks.

We drove for nearly three hundred kilometres north from Makassar to reach Toraja country. At first the road was excellent, running in a straight line across the flat paddy fields of the wide coastal plain. Little thatched houses of the seafaring Bugis people with Saint Andrew's crosses at the beam ends, and every now and then a small clump of trees, broke the monotony of the landscape. Water buffalo and small brown cows grazed at the roadside, while goats, ducks and chickens were herded on the stubbles of the freshly-cut rice. Several houses had large domesticated deer, occasionally with young, wandering free in the gardens; a familiar sight in many parts of Indonesia, and one which must indicate that their potential as a source of food, in parts of the world where the terrain is not suitable for other stock, cannot have been properly explored yet. Fine sailing ships, the Bugis' *praus*, with one or two masts and white sails flapping, were visible through the trees on the banks of the rivers, which we usually crossed by shaky plank bridges with gangs of men working to repair them before they collapsed under the weight of the next overcrowded bus. Far on our right was a range of craggy limestone rocks and hills, which slowly crept nearer to the coast, providing a romantic and startling background to the bright greens and yellows of the rice fields, like the distant scenes in a painting by Leonardo da Vinci.

It was hot driving across the plain and along the seashore, where palm trees and mangrove swamps lined the road further north, but at Pare Pare we turned inland and began to climb up into the mountains. For mile after mile we now passed through rolling dry grassland, cattle country with wide views and a burnt savannah atmosphere quite unlike anything we had seen in the other islands. Soon the road deteriorated and we had to cling to our seats as the jeep bumped over successive ranges of hills, separating more open plains. It was hard to believe that any country could be even more beautiful than all we had seen on the way, but although it was becoming dark as we passed under the carved arch after Enrekang, which marks the entrance to the land of the Toraja, and although it began to rain so that we could only see glimpses of the landscape, we knew at once that we had reached somewhere magical and fantastic.

As with the Bataks at Lake Toba in Sumatra, the threat of tourism hangs over Tana Toraja in the centre of Celebes. When the road is completed, halving the present driving time from Makassar of about twelve hours, increasing numbers will be sure to arrive; and this is hardly surprising as it is one of the most beautiful and fascinating places in the world, rivalling Kashmir in scenic grandeur and Batakland in the picturesqueness of its architecture and the charm of its rural life. It is also one of the few places in the world which I have seen where man's impact on the landscape has not only improved it by the addition of attractive houses, but has also enhanced its aesthetic appeal by major physical alterations. In order to make paddy fields for growing wet rice on the steep mountainsides, the Toraja have sculpted and terraced every available slope, creating a myriad gentle waves along the contours, bands of contrasting greens, through which the streams originating near the hilltops have been harnessed to flow in a dazzling succession of tiny waterfalls before escaping once more into the wild natural riverbeds where, released from all control, the water seems to rush and tumble with renewed energy. Whenever an acre of naturally flat land occurs, whether on the high shoulder of a mountain or deep in a valley where the rivers run smoothly, clumps of trees and bamboos screen clusters of houses, their curved roofs soaring gracefully towards the sky. It seems inconceivable that such a timeless scenario could have been created in a bare sixty years and yet, although the architecture of the houses has not changed for centuries, before the arrival of the Dutch, we are told that the Toraja grew their crops by slash and burn agriculture, hunting and gathering produce in the now largely vanished forests and grazing their buffalo herds on the bare hillsides.

Near to the market town of Rantepao, where the Toraja bring their produce for sale, we visited the small village of Palawa. Two rows of half a dozen houses faced each other, dwelling houses on one side and rice stores on the other. The first impression one receives on walking into a Toraja village is amazement at the sheer size and extravagance of the roofs. Built of thousands of matched pieces of bamboo, laid one upon the other like roof tiles, they sweep up in a great curve to a point, like the prow of a ship, at either end, and although the central 'street' is in reality quite wide, they give the impression of almost meeting in the centre as though one were on a river with the trees spreading overhead. There is a much disputed legend that the design of the houses reflects an ancient folk memory of the ships in which the distant ancestors of the Toraja arrived, sailing perhaps from

China by way of Japan and the Philippines. Standing on thick solid piles the rectangular body of the house is small in contrast to the roof, consisting of two or three dark rooms with low doors and windows. The whole building is massively constructed of hard wood, no metal nails being used, but the whole being securely slotted and pegged together. If necessary, a house can be moved bodily by placing the piles on runners and pushing it to a new site. Outside, every visible expanse of wood is painted or carved in strong colours; red, white, black and yellow are favoured, and the pattern designs are often surmounted by a pair of dried buffalo horns. The houses must be built facing north which, as they are in the southern hemisphere, means that the sun usually strikes directly onto the narrow balcony over the entrance. Beneath one of these we found an old lady weaving brightly coloured rugs, and we were glad to buy a couple as the nights are cold and damp in the mountains.

High above the valley, after a tortuous drive along a rough track which taxed the jeep to its limits, we reached Riew, an almost alpine plateau with a view out over a dizzy drop of more than a thousand metres, to the ranges of rugged, forested mountains in the distance. Here the road ended and we walked some way to Lokomata where a gigantic boulder, the size of an office block, had hollowed tombs carved into it. Each had its own carved wooden door, sealing off the entrance, some old and rotten, some new and freshly painted. They were high above the ground and to reach them we would have needed scaffolding or a ladder, but we were not tempted to linger in any case as one of the graves had been occupied by a swarm of large vicious hornets, which made it quite clear that close inspection was not welcome. Nearby was an impressive stone circle, the monoliths rising up four metres high and surrounding a big rock like a sacrificial altar in the middle. We had glimpsed several of these henges on our way up the mountain in the early morning mist, and no one seemed to know a lot about their origins. They still play an important part in Toraja ritual, buffaloes being slaughtered there when great men die, and they apparently mark the sites of the old pre-conquest fortified villages. Stones are still very occasionally dragged out of the rice fields and added to the circles as a memorial to a dead chief, but most are old and weathered, looking as though they have been standing for centuries.

While there, we heard enchanting music carried to us by the wind from a house some way below. Intrigued, we went down to the house and found that it was a school in which some forty children were playing a variety of bamboo wind instruments under the instruction of their teacher, who tapped out the rhythm on a blackboard. Most of the boys, ranging from teenagers to little tackers of no more than four or five, had unusual double pipes which some were able to blow into two at a time. They were accompanied by a row of girls with high pitched flutes and a virtuoso older boy who played the melody, also on a flute. The result was a delightfully gay harmony, very much alpine mountain music, and, in fact, their teacher was a well-known Toraja musician who had been to Jakarta to play for the President.

The landscape of Toraja country provides a constant succession of breathtaking views. When the mist clears from the deep valleys and the clouds drift off the jagged mountains, the air is fresh and the light intense so that sounds carry over great distances. Smoke rises from the clumps of tall bamboos, betraying the presence of close-knit villages hidden within them. Everywhere terraces sweep and curve down the slopes. Water is carried in narrow channels or in bamboo pipes on stilts without any waste so that it does its work of irrigating and carrying nutrients to the soil again and again. Many of the little plots were no more than a few metres long and no wider than a flowerbed, and yet each is religiously cultivated with single furrow ploughs, pulled by patient, lumbering black water buffaloes. When flooded to a depth of a few centimetres to cause the rice to germinate, small freshwater fish are introduced which are speared by little boys with sharp sticks when they have fattened sufficiently. These fish play an important rôle in the Toraja economy, providing a valuable source of protein. Recently, as a result of an ill-conceived agricultural experiment promoted by an international agency, pesticides were sprayed from an aircraft on certain hillsides in order to improve the rice crop. Instead the fish all died as well as several Toraja who drank the water carried off the fields.

It was market day in Rantepao, and the road was crowded with people carrying loads of vegetables and bulging sacks, or driving cattle or a single squealing piglet tied by the hind leg to a long string. Everyone wanted a lift and the jeep was soon grossly overcrowded so that our patient driver, Asrad, who came from Makassar and regarded the Toraja as suspect and probably dangerous, began to look worried about his chances of ever reaching home again.

The megalithic culture of the Toraja shares a common feature with others to be found in Nias and Flores in possessing a deep preoccupation with life after death. The stone circles and associated sacrifices of buffaloes are designed to protect the soul of the departed on his journey while at the same time providing a visible link with the ancestors so as to encourage them to maintain an interest in their descendants' future prosperity. The sacrifices, ceremonies and feasts, which in the case of the Toraja often last for months on end, are not so much designed to satisfy the mourners or furnish symbolic food for the deceased as to impress the gods whom he will be joining with his importance so that he will be able to intercede effectively on their behalf. There is a most readable book about life among the Toraja of the region of Rantepao by an Englishman called Henry Willcox. It is called *White Stranger, Six Moons in Celebes,* published in 1949, and was the first English description of them. In it Willcox says that funerals were almost continuous during his stay, although the other great festivals and ceremonies were beginning to die out. Now funerals, too, are rarer as Christian and Muslim rituals replace them.

We were fortunate in being able to attend a Toraja funeral one day in a village some distance from any road, up a steep footpath leading into the hills through dense undergrowth. The dead man, though not a great chief, had been a man of some importance and about three hundred people had gathered to pay their respects to him. Three buffaloes, several pigs and a few chickens had already been slaughtered and eaten during the preceding days. In the past, when a big funeral took place, so many buffaloes were killed that almost none were left to breed from and the Government had had to step in and discourage the practice. Almost the first thing we saw as we entered the village was the severed head of a buffalo, displayed beneath one of the houses. A crowd of men and women sat in groups chatting and laughing in a thoroughly festive atmosphere. Most of the women wore black dresses, while the men were either in sarongs, locally called *sambu*, or wore shirts and trousers with the *sambu* draped over their shoulders. Almost everyone was chewing betel and the ground was streaked with the marks of crimson spittle. From a room in the main house came the sound of wailing, and we went in to view the body which was tightly wrapped in layers of coloured cloth, neatly sewn at the ends to make a regular shape like a bolster. This was laid across forked trestles with the corpse's hat hung on one of the uprights, while around it half a dozen women buried their faces in their hands and keened loudly. As is usual with Toraja funerals, the man had died some three months before and we were witnessing the culmination of a series of rituals, after which the body would be laid to rest in the depths of a limestone cave.

More people were arriving for the ceremony, each carrying a green bamboo tube filled with palm wine (*tuak*) which the Toraja make from a tree called *induk*. While Marika rested and joined in the general sampling of the wine, I went further up the hill to see the cliff where the graves were. In front of this, in an open meadow, a platform had been erected where the body would later be placed and everyone would dance around it. Climbing up the almost sheer rock wall, where thorny bushes grew out of crevices, I reached the holes cut into the cliff face and looked in. Piles of human bones and skulls lay heaped together, bleached white. Further along there was a ledge on which stood a row of fifteen roughly carved wooden figures with, in front of them, a much more lifelike effigy of a man with painted eyes, wearing a white robe and with what I took to be a miner's helmet on his head. Perhaps this was a Toraja who had gone away to work at a factory on the coast, and returned to be buried with his ancestors, but no one there knew his history. It was a quiet, peaceful place with the white cliffs towering up to the blue sky above and a flock of white cockatoos swooping below from tree to tree.

Back in the village, the bier had been carried outside the house and, while the women continued to keen beside it, a group of male friends and relations linked their little fingers and performed a jerky, swaying dance in a half circle. Meanwhile, cooked meats and rice were passed around on dishes made of palm leaves, and we all had a hearty meal washed down with fresh tubes of *tuak*. Later, trays of tobacco and strips of paper were brought out, from which all were invited to roll their own cigarettes. The old servant of the dead man, who had been eighty when he died, stopped the chatter from time to time to chant a eulogy in praise of his master, reciting his deeds of valour and his good work. Then everyone went back to eating again. We walked round to the open air kitchen behind the house to watch how the meat and giblets, with green plants and blood, were packed into yet more bamboo tubes and then cooked in the fire. Another pig was killed, presumably because more guests than expected had turned up; the entrails were carefully removed and examined before being cleaned and packed away, but the body of the pig was slung on a pole and carried off towards the burial cliff where, we were informed, it would be roasted later. It began to rain and everyone crowded under the houses for shelter. The bier was carried back indoors and, since it seemed unlikely that much more would happen that day, we thanked all the people who had accepted our presence in a most refreshing and easygoing way, and slithered off down the now muddy and precipitous mountainside.

Not far off the main road, at a place called Londa, we saw another burial cliff where the caves reached far back into the rock for a mile or more, and where wooden coffins, old and new, were stacked on ledges and piled in heaps. More carved figures stood in a row above the entrance, and there was an attractive replica of a Toraja house which is carried in procession at funerals. One had taken place only a few days before and the freshly made coffin lay with the others. About forty per cent of the Toraja are now Christians, unlike almost all the other peoples of southern Sulawesi, who are predominately Muslim. The remainder of the Toraja are unashamedly animist. Although it is one of the five articles of the Indonesian constitution that every citizen must observe a faith in only one God, they have recently had their beliefs officially sanctioned, thanks to their being a fairly powerful and influential group with several Toraja in quite high government offices. The formula under which this was allowed suggested that their traditions were similar to those of the Balinese Hindus, for whom an exception is also made—a tenuous connection to say the least. However, their religion clearly thrives and, with it, their traditions and ceremonies, their art and artifacts, and their superb houses with their ritually preserved design, and graphic decorations and symbolism. But what will happen when progress, in the form of main roads and tourism, modern factories and technology, reach them? No people as energetic and productive as the Toraja can be insulated from the outside world, and there is no indication that they would wish this to happen. The Toraja are prosperous. They grow a surplus of rice, which is exported, and excellent coffee of a type called *bungin*, which is much sought after and brings them in a substantial income. Already, modern houses are appearing around Rantepao and corrugated iron roofs are replacing bamboo ones in the same way as is happening with the Bataks. One cannot help wondering what will happen when the new tourist hotels, now planned, are finally built. We encountered an example of one of the undesirable effects when we visited an attractive village called Marante, a few kilometres from Rantepao, and accessible by a good road. The people seemed sullen and unfriendly by contrast to those we had met and been welcomed by further away in the mountains. The Headman sidled up to us as we stood admiring one of the houses, and trying to photograph the carvings on the façade. 'You must pay a thousand rupiahs, (about one pound)' he said. I asked him what he meant. He looked shifty and embarrassed. 'Well how about five hundred?' he persisted. 'Have you anything to sell?' I asked, but there was no one in the village weaving or carving the decorated boxes we had seen elsewhere, and I explained, rather pompously, that although I would be happy to support local industry I could not encourage him to beg. Of course, it must be unsatisfactory to have strangers coming into your village, gawping at your houses and photographing everything you do. It is only right that the Toraja themselves should be the first to benefit from a tourist industry when it develops, rather than the entrepreneurs who build the hotels. But the sad fact is that a tourist presence almost inevitably cheapens and eventually eliminates the very things which attracted them in the first place. How to overcome this disturbing process is a subject which is taxing better brains than mine, and I only hope answers can be found which will help the Toraja to preserve their dignity and pride before it is too late. In one sense, the only people who can solve the problems bearing down on them are the Toraja themselves and, being a tough, resilient people, they may well prove capable of doing so. But in another sense beauty, such as they have created in an idyllic setting supplied by nature, belongs to the whole world, and they should be given every encouragement to protect it.

Toana

In search of simpler people, with problems more easy to identify, we travelled on to the head of Bone bay where we had heard that there was a tribe of sea nomads called Bajo. They were said to be very shy and retiring, living in small boats in the creeks and swamps of the edge of the sea, and avoiding contact with people on the shore. I was told a confused legend about a great king from Java who had sailed all over the world. One day, on the coast of Celebes, he cut down a huge tree to build a new boat. It fell into the sea, making a great wave which flooded the land and drowned many people. After this, the survivors decided it was safer to live afloat, going ashore as seldom as possible; and this was the origin of the tribe. We never found them, and some said that they had all moved away further down the coast; but the search was not wasted as it gave us a chance to see another part of Celebes and brought me rumours of other tribes whom I hope to contact one day.

The road from Rantepao to Palopo climbs steeply to a pass where both the vegetation and the populace change abruptly. At the top, pinewoods cover the slopes, with palm trees and bamboo groves blending with them from below. To the north stretches wild, barely penetrable country of high mountains into which no roads lead. Celebes is a transitional region between Asian and Australian flora and fauna, and some of the wildlife is like none other to be found elsewhere in the world. Among these are the *babirusa*, a strange long-legged creature with tusks which curve upwards like horns and led to its confusing name which means pig-deer. It is, in fact, a rather large, wild, almost hairless grey pig and it is also found on the island of Buru. There is also the now quite rare *anoa,* a wild, dwarf buffalo which looks more like a small, dark brown Jersey cow, being little more than three feet high and having sharp, straight horns, than the heavy black creatures that we saw working in the rice fields. Although they can be vicious when attacked, they are shy, retiring creatures and have been driven deep into the interior by hunting and the destruction of their habitat.

On the other side of the pass we stopped to look out over an endless vista of thick green tropical jungle, rolling down to the coast. Across the water we could see the mountains on the far side of Bone bay, over one hundred kilometres away. No more rice paddies or cleared land here, but only the hum of a million insects in the undergrowth, and a sheer sided gorge down which the road corkscrewed out of sight. The few houses we passed belonged to Muslim subsistence farmers, who grew a few ragged crops on the hills near them and sat by the roadside with baskets of wild fruit for sale. As we only passed one decrepit bus and a petrol tanker on the whole drive, we felt that much of their time must be spent waiting in vain.

It was particularly hot and raining again when we reached Palopo which made the squalid, empty and run-down doss house even less inviting; in spite of its name, *Rio Rita,* which means 'pleasant stay' in Buginese, it could hardly be called an hotel. But things looked better when we went to call on the Bupati (the senior civil administrator of a district). His name was Galib Lasahido and he was a kind and charming man, interested in our plan and willing to help us in every way. We asked him about isolated, indigenous tribes in his district. The words for this are as difficult and imprecise in Indonesian as they are in English, but the nearest equivalent is *orang* (meaning 'man'), *asli* (meaning 'original' or 'aboriginal'). He said the only ones he knew of lived near a place called Limbang, several days' walk from the road head, far to the north. Although it would be impossible for us to reach them in the time we had, it so happened that their Rajah was in Palopo and he would send for him. The old man, when he arrived, was introduced to us as Tomo Kaka Patuang, and with him was his son, a cheerful young man in his twenties. He told us that his people were called the Suku Ronkong, and that in 1954 there had been seventeen thousand of them, but that their numbers had been reduced to about eight thousand today through migration to the coast in search of work. Most of those who had stayed were now settled agriculturists, but some were still hunters using bows and arrows and blowpipes to hunt *babirusa* and *anoa*. They lived on a high plateau, seventy kilometres long by ten kilometres wide, which an archaeologist had told him was once the bed of a lake, and it was higher and colder there than at Rantepao in Tana Toraja. It is scrub country up there, but the lower slopes are covered in dense jungle; the houses are round and there are two very old ones left which he thought might be three hundred years old; his people used to tattoo themselves and have long hair, but this is disappearing except among the Suku Tolampung, the most isolated group, who have very white skin and consist of about seventy families. Unlike the rest, these have not been converted to Christianity or Islam, but they are hard to reach, living ten days' ride by horse away from the road across very difficult country. The Rajah, himself, now spends most of his time in Palopo, and he said that no foreigner had visited his people since a Dutch anthropologist worked there in 1937. There are two other tribes in the same region, each with a separate language and their own Rajah; the Lampung, whose Rajah is called Tobara; and the Rampi, with a Rajah by the name of Tokoi. The Rampi had a peculiar custom whereby adults pull out all their teeth. It was said to be a punishment for some grave crime that the tribe had once committed. The Dutch banned this in 1939 so that today only the old people are toothless.

At this point I produced a copy of my book on the Indians of Brazil, which I had with me, and the Rajah became very excited by the pictures. He pointed at the long, bass flutes used by some of the Xingu tribes and said that some of his people had similar ones, but only played them on very special occasions. Then he spotted a man with large plugs through his earlobes. His tribe, too, had once pierced their ears, but the practice was dying out; the feather headdresses were immediately familiar to him and so were grass skirts and the whole gamut of ceremonial regalia. It was with a strange feeling of unreality that I watched him turning the pages and nodding with pleasure and evident recognition over pictures of totally unrelated peoples from the other side of the world. He launched into a series of complicated stories about the magic practised by various tribes, involving the power to disappear and to catch the *anoa* through becoming invisible, but the Bupati interrupted his flow as it was becoming very late, time for us all to go to bed. Since it was clearly out of the question for us to reach the Rajah's territory and return in under a week, the Bupati suggested, to our astonishment since we had never dared hope for such generosity, that we borrow his fast, motorized canoe for a few days in order to visit the far side of the bay. Perhaps, he said, we might find some traces of the sea nomads after all. Having ascertained that we could both swim, as he warned us that the sea could be rough and the boat was small, he sent us off to bed, saying that his boatman would be ready to leave at eight the following morning. This was, perhaps, the most extreme example of the luck and kindness which made it possible for us to cover so much ground in such a short time.

The canoe was one metre wide by ten metres long, with outriggers and a forty horsepower motor. Not knowing how long we would be away for, we instructed Asrad to wait with the jeep on the quay each day from twelve until three, and headed out to sea until land was only a faint blur on the horizon to the north. Our objective was Malili, the base and company town for a large multinational consortium working a nickel mine further inland. There, we hoped to learn if any of the engineers or prospectors had come across the people we sought. The motor never faltered and we entered the Malili river six hours after leaving Palopo. There had once been a thriving settlement at Malili, built by the Dutch, but this was largely destroyed by the Japanese during the war. The rusty hulks of sunken ships testified to the fighting that had taken place then. However, no sooner was the war over, and Indonesian independence declared, than Malili had the misfortune of becoming the chief rebel stronghold in Celebes so that it was repeatedly razed and burnt during the 1950s and 1960s until virtually nothing was left. Only in the last couple of years had prosperity miraculously arrived again, in the form of Inco, the nickel company, who had built a complete air-conditioned town for their employees on the hill overlooking what remained of the old town. And so it was that after a day spent in a fragile canoe, often out of sight of land and with virtually no chance of being rescued if we capsized; after being broiled in the fierce sun for hour after hour, and caked with rime from the sea spray; after nosing our way through the mangrove swamps at the mouth of a silent, green, mysterious river, we suddenly found ourselves sitting beside an immaculate tennis court, sipping long iced drinks, and watching an Australian, an Indonesian, a Chinaman and an Englishman play in the men's doubles Inco-Malili cup.

Staying in the cool, bachelor mess eating tins of processed, imported food, made a refreshing change. I was solemnly warned that when Marika used the wash house I should stand outside to keep guard as, apart from a handful of company wives, the camp was all male. After fending for ourselves for so long, we felt almost stiflingly protected in the compound, insulated from the outside world by a high barbed-wire fence, in an environment where English was the *lingua franca,* and the daily flight of the company 'plane to Makassar the lifeline to civilization. We were generously lent a Landrover and driver, warned to watch out for snakes and reassured that if we were not back by nightfall a search party would be sent out to look for us. Since nothing was known of any *orang asli* in the neighbourhood, we drove up the recently completed company road; a considerable engineering achievement, which sliced its way up the wild Larona gorge across an open area of savannah country and down to Lake Matano. The rebel leader, Kahar Muzakar, had held out near there with the remnant of his army for fifteen years, hiding in caves in the hills. On New Year's Day 1966, they had all come down to a village for a celebration, where they had been trapped and finished off by Indonesian army paratroops.

On the edge of Lake Matano we stopped at a comfortable Inco camp where the company was planning to build a new town for the fifteen thousand workers needed to develop the nickel mine. They provided us with a boat so that we could go along the lake shore to see some burial caves which had recently been discovered. The lake is the deepest in Indonesia, having been sounded to five hundred and ninety metres. It lies at four hundred metres above sea level so that the bottom is nearly two hundred metres below sea level. Since the water is also quite exceptionally clear, pale blue, and almost entirely free of algae, we could see far down through the depth to the rocks below. It was more like being in an aeroplane than in a boat. The caves were in the side of a cliff, hidden behind a curtain of vegetation. We scrambled up, using lianas as handholds, and found an entrance with a few broken pots lying outside. The boatman warned us again about snakes, but we had brought a torch and crept nervously inside. A great heap of bones, skulls and rotting coffins confronted us. Beyond them, the floor sloped sharply upwards towards a distant shaft of light, while on one side there was a dark chasm at the bottom of which we could see water. Edging past this we began to find large numbers of pots, many of them unbroken, as well as strings of bronze bracelets, and a few heavy bronze pots. While Marika picked these over, looking for inscriptions, I went on further, giving myself a nasty fright when, on turning a corner and feeling as one does in caves very much alone, I shone the torch upwards where thousands of little red eyes were staring down at me. With a great rushing of wings, a multitude of bats took off and swooped around the cave, fluttering and squeaking. Deciding that exploring caves was probably best left to speliologists, I retreated to the entrance. Marika had found a pot with 'made in Holland 1836 by P. Regout at Maastricht' on the base, as well as some fairly fresh clothes near a coffin which looked relatively new so that it seemed likely that the place had been used for burial in the not too distant past. One day it will probably be excavated properly but, as the boatman expressed nervousness about offending the spirits and was anxious to leave, we took nothing and climbed back down. The motor, which had been giving trouble on the way, suddenly cleared as we left, at which he looked more cheerful saying that that was a sign that all was well and we had been forgiven our intrusion.

At dinner that night one of the research geologists told us a story which made me prick my ears up. Inco had been granted a concession to prospect over the whole of eastern Sulawesi, the shortest of the four peninsulas forming the island of Celebes, but the least explored. It was, he said, a sparsely populated area with only a few fishing villages around the coast, difficult mountains, forested country with scattered clearings here and there inland. Using helicopters, teams had flown into these clearings to collect mineral specimens and assess the mining potential and, in particular, the presence of nickel throughout the peninsula. From the air, the prospectors had seen little sign of human habitation in the interior; an occasional cluster of thatched huts and one or two small patches under cultivation, but no indication that the rest of the land contained any people at all. But each time a helicopter landed, and it was their job to cover as much as possible of the interior, people would arrive within an hour or so. Once of twice arrows had been fired, but no one had ever been hit, and they had seemed to be warning shots, deliberately wide of the mark. Much more often the people had emerged from the surrounding cover and made a friendly approach. They had been short and dark, with long curly hair and broad, flat noses. The men wore bark loin cloths and the women had been bare-breasted. They carried blowpipes and attractively decorated quivers containing poisoned darts, as well as narrow shields with a knob on the front. Very shy and liable to run off if alarmed, they had usually arrived in parties of about twenty, asking for salt for which they readily exchanged anything they had with them. One of the pilots had acquired some of the darts and had later experimented with one, pricking a stray dog with it. The dog had died within ten minutes.

Known locally as Toanas, which was said to mean bush people, and in Indonesian as Tokala meaning 'lost people', they may be the same as the Toala, who are often referred to as the true aborigines of Celebes, and were probably Negritos, but have now mostly vanished through being absorbed or exterminated by later arrivals. Considerable discussion developed when I asked how many of them there were thought to be. Through the regularity with which they had been seen over a wide area, it was felt that there must be several thousand wandering as nomads in small groups. They travelled to the coast from time to time to trade for salt, but normally remained hidden in the mountains, which rose to over seven thousand feet along the central ridge. Some had settled along a river running into the north coast and the local Bupati had sent some expeditions to try and persuade the rest to move down to the sea shore, where they could be 'civilized', but he had been rebuffed. His estimate of their numbers was said to be sixteen thousand, but this was thought to be an exaggeration.

Inco had ceased prospecting in eastern Sulawesi a short while before, having found no minerals worth exploiting and, in fact, their concession to the area had lapsed. This may have been good news for the Toanas, but was sad for us, particularly when the geologists said that, had the helicopters still been there, we would have been welcome to go along for the ride on some of the surveys. I resolved that, if possible, I would return one day and make contact with the Toanas, perhaps walking the length of the peninsula so as to gain an idea of their number. Sooner or later some other scheme, if not based on minerals, then on timber extraction or oil or agriculture, will be dreamt up for the development of their lands. Unless something is known about them before such proposals are submitted, their interests will almost certainly be overlooked, with the usual disastrous results. Far better that they should be given the chance to have a say in their own destiny so that, at the least, they can attempt to benefit from whatever occurs by establishing their rights to the land and (faint hope) its resources while, at the same time, contributing their own unique knowledge of its environment; or, at best, the implications of whatever changes were planned could be explained to them so that they could choose their own rôle in future events. In this way, unlike so many other tribes of hunter gatherers throughout the world which have vanished, they might survive. Whatever the final cause of extinction of a group, whether they succumbed to new diseases to which they had no resistance like the otherwise astonishingly hardy Yahgan Indians of Tierra del Fuego or whether they were deliberately hunted and killed like some of the bushman clans of Africa, without their land they never really stood a chance. Few, if any, such peoples have been successfully assimilated into another race without appalling suffering. If the Toana are to be spared this, the first step must be to secure their right to at least some of their land before others take it from them. Survival International should, I thought, definitely develop an interest in them, but this was not the time for us to undertake that sort of investigation. There was no way of reaching eastern Sulawesi quickly and even a superficial visit would take weeks. Meanwhile, our jeep was waiting in Palopo and so was the long drive back to Makassar.

Tana Towa

❧

IN Makassar we had met a remarkable man. Doctor Meyer had been a doctor in the German army at the outbreak of the Second World War. Captured in 1944 by the Russians, he had spent the next five years as a prisoner in Siberia, surviving indescribable hardships only by a series of miracles, helped along by his value to his captors as a doctor, and his indomitable good spirits. After the war he had given up the chance of a lucrative practice in Germany and emigrated to Sulawesi, where he had devoted his life to surgery in the appallingly understaffed medical service. Often, he was the only doctor capable of major surgery, working in turn in each of the three hospitals—Government, Protestant and Catholic. He had travelled over much of the island and was known and admired everywhere. As with many excessively busy men, his interest and enthusiasm ranged far beyond the confines of this particular discipline. Cultural minorities fascinated him, and he took an immediate interest in Survival International. On our way through Makassar he had advised us on where to go, generously suggesting areas of possible interest and giving us introductions to people in the most unlikely places. Above all, he said that there was a community about a day's drive from Makassar which he had long wished to visit and where he believed no European had ever been. 'Let's see what happens when you get back' was all he would say before we drove north to the Toraja and beyond, but on our return we found that he had made all the arrangements to take a few days off from his work and travel with us, so that almost before we had had time to have a bath and arrange for our clothes to be washed at the rundown old *Grand Hotel,* we were setting off again, this time towards the south-east.

I had read something about a similar sect in Bantam province in west Java called the Badui—there is an excellent short description of them in Peter Polomka's book, *Indonesia Since Sukarno*, published by Pelican in 1971—but have never seen a reference before or since to the people of Tana Towa. The Badui are quite well-known and, in their way, powerful although they too have banned outsiders from their territory since an incident in the early part of the century when some Dutchmen had attempted to excavate their sacred megaliths before being driven out. They have three 'inner' villages where all the people dress in white robes, and a strict way of life is observed, the use of ornaments and objects made by outsiders being prohibited. Around them lies a buffer zone of 'black' Badui, dressed in indigo, who have compromised with the modern world to some extent, talking to strangers, practising commerce and even travelling to Jakarta from time to time. Their power and influence rests in the respect which the Javanese have for their mystic abilities as oracles and suppliers of potent talismans as, in particular, daggers (*kris*) which are cherished by most men of influence from the President down. Tana Towa fulfils the same rôle for Sulawesi.

Doctor Meyer regaled us, on the long drive, with a constant stream of hilarious, bawdy and sometimes horrific stories; his experiences on the Russian front in the terrible winters of 1943 and 1944 when the troops on both sides had resorted to cannibalism; the skill with which Rumanian gypsies had managed to make even life in the salt mines of Siberia bearable and interesting; his relationship with the eccentric Daisy O'Keefe, the last surviving daughter of the legendary O'Keefe of the South Seas, who had trained as a ballet dancer in Shanghai, become the mistress of half the crowned heads of Europe, and retired to spend the last fifteen years of her life as a grand old lady in Makassar and who had died a few months before; lurid legends about the *pok pok*, a Sulawesi spirit, which comes down the chimney at night and enters unsuspecting bodies by any available orifice, so that the person becomes possessed, as well as the many cases he had had reported to him of twins being born, one of which was a baby crocodile which would then be released into the river, grow to enormous size and remain a friend of the family. Even when some petrol was accidentally spilled over his leg, and he was quite severely burned, he barely paused in the anecdote he was telling, so that the journey sped past. The fourth member of our party was a silent French anthropologist called Christian Pelras, who took copious notes of everything we saw from house design to agricultural practices. He was making a study of the Bugis, and his fluency in their difficult language was of constant value.

After a night en route we reached the town of Kadjang, on the east coast, where Doctor Meyer was immediately recognized as the man who had saved the life of the *camat*'s wife, thereby giving us a flying start in our negotiations for permission to enter Tana Towa. But even the *camat* had to seek the consent of the people themselves and so, while messengers were dispatched, we drove south to Bira, a pretty little port at the very tip of southern Sulawesi, to look at some of the famous Bugis' *praus*, which are built there. We saw one under construction, the wooden planks accurately shaped with an adze by rule of thumb, and the boat fashioned from the outside in without an inner frame. The sight of a row of two-masted *praus*, moored off a golden beach with a coral islet and the endless open sea behind, could not fail to lift the dullest spirit and fill one with admiration for the compulsive, fearless sailors, who have sailed for centuries to every corner of the eastern seas, guided by little more than their own instincts and a white cockerel penned in the bow to warn of approaching reefs.

Permission seemed unlikely to be granted for us to enter the inner circle of Tana Towa, but ponies were provided on which we rode to Possitana, one of their sacred places, the navel of the earth. At the top of a steep ridge, between the sea and a great hazy plain stretching inland, we were greeted by the keeper of the sacred stones. Several large grey boulders, some with inscriptions and carved geometric figures on them, lay along the ridge. Each had its own legend; that it had appeared miraculously from heaven after the death of a great Rajah; or contained the spirit of one of the peoples' ancestors. The most important stones—two heavy flat slabs surrounded by a well-kept double bamboo fence, and with the earth around freshly swept bare—marked the navel, itself. Beneath the slabs there was said to be a hole leading straight to the sea, about a thousand feet below. Human sacrifices took place here in the not too distant past, but today they probably only use buffaloes and chickens. So little is known about the Tana Towa, and the local people surround them with such intense mystique and reverence, that one can do little more than speculate.

On the third day, when we had just about given up hope and were planning to return to Makassar, word came that we were to be allowed to go to the heart of Tana Towa and that ponies were waiting to take us from a village on the road called Kalimpero. During the wait we had been treated with excessive hospitality, being fed lavishly on rice, meat and hot spices at all hours. Although we had just had breakfast with the *camat* of Katjang, the headman of Kalimpero insisted that we once more sat down in his house to another generous spread before we were allowed to set off. The ponies were fast, but thin and ridged-backed. They had no saddles or stirrups, just a hard little pad which soon moulded itself to the horse's spine so that, after a short time, riding them felt like sitting astride a metal gate attached to a pneumatic drill. However, our excitement was such that we barely noticed the discomfort on the outward journey, urging our mounts to gallop which was, in any case, considerably easier on the behind.

As soon as we entered Tana Towa the atmosphere changed dramatically. At first we only noticed the blessed relief of being away from the inevitable crowd of noisy, shouting children, who had accompanied us everywhere in the coastal villages. Here, people were quiet and dignified, the children well-mannered and friendly, while the adults seemed barely aware of our passing. Then we began to notice the silence and the peace. A man was ploughing a rice field behind his ox; a woman passed carrying a string of round gourds slung on a pole; another sat on the steps of her house weaving. All wore clothes of deep indigo blue or black. The cotton must be grown, woven and made up in Tana Towa, itself; nothing may be introduced from the outside world. The men's shirts were like bush-jackets with short sleeves, pockets sewn on the front and round collars; below this, all wore sarongs or, as they should more properly be called, when worn by men, *salendangs*. The women's clothes were darker, often shiny black with a rather chic blouse over an ankle-length sarong. Their faces were sharp and ascetic, with high cheek bones and fine features; many of the men had moustaches, and they walked with confidence and grace. The houses, too, were quite different, built according to the traditional pattern. High up in the trees, beside the narrow track along which we rode, were little huts on platforms where children were sent to spend the night when the fruit was ripening, banging gongs and clapping to frighten away the flocks of fruit-eating bats which would otherwise strip the trees before the fruit could be gathered.

After a couple of hours hard riding we reached the central inner village of Tana Towa called Benteng, meaning 'fortress' in Indonesian. It consisted of a few houses, grouped around an open-sided shelter on stilts, where guests were accommodated and meetings took place. There, we tied up our horses and sat down cross-legged on mats to wait. The *jaksa* or magistrate of Katjang, who had himself been born in Tana Towa and so spoke their special language—an archaic form of Makassarese called Conjo which Christian Pelras, for all his knowledge of Bugis, could not understand—had come with us to act as interpreter. While we waited he told us more about the customs and history of the community. Tana Towa means 'old country' and the *adat* has changed little for three thousand years. Originally, there were no houses in the world. The first house appeared miraculously near to where we were sitting, its uprights made of chili wood which was then a tall tree, not just a little plant as it has since become. This house, which had been carefully preserved, had served as the model for all later houses. Man had also originated here, and every rock and tree, the very ground itself, was sacred. Early in the seventeenth century, Islam had been brought to southern Sulawesi from Sumatra. The ruler of Tana Towa had sent his three sons to study the whole religion, who had returned and taught it to their father. Now the people were officially Muslim like the surrounding population, but their own religion was older and stronger and, although many, including Christian missionaries, had tried to change them, none had had any success. 'We are already Muslim,' they said with irrefutable logic, 'but our own beliefs encompass much more and so we cannot be changed.' At one time, fanatical young Muslims from outside had come and rolled some of the great stones at Possitana down the hill, but they had returned overnight of their own accord.

The ruler of Tana Towa is called the *Ama Towa*, a holy man chosen only after an elaborate series of strict tests and miraculous events. These are so rigorous that after the last one died in 1948 there was a gap of seventeen years before another was found worthy. He must be a man of exceptional purity and wisdom, and yet he must never have set foot outside the inner zone. He must be able to foretell the future, and when he sleeps he must be seen to levitate above his bed. He must be married and may have children which, to Marika and my irreverent minds, seemed to pose certain problems if he always passed the nights in mid-air, and on the day of the final ceremony at which he is chosen and appointed *Ama Towa* certain supernatural events have to take place. The council of elders sit in a circle and a fire is lit in the centre. A chicken is released which must go and peck for food at his feet. A buffalo, which was turned loose in the jungle a week before, must return of its own accord at the appointed hour and walk up to him. It is then sacrificed and placed on the fire when the smoke must drift in his direction and envelop him.

Many people want to meet the *Ama Towa* and seek his advice. A few weeks before, a party of high-ranking generals had come from Makassar to consult him. For three days they had sat in the shelter at Benteng, but no audience had been granted. We were the first Europeans to be allowed that far and no one knew what would happen. In an atmosphere charged with anticipation we sat and waited. The *jaksa* said that we must not take any photographs if the *Ama Towa* appeared; and then, walking in single file down the path towards us, came eleven men. They looked like monks in immaculate dark blue robes with turbans of the same colour on their heads, tied in a peculiar way so that the ends stood up in points like an admiral's hat. We all moved to one end of the meeting house as they came up the steps and one, unmistakably the *Ama Towa*, was escorted with deference to the finest mat and the rest grouped themselves around him. One by one we went forward and, following the *jaksa*'s example, took his right hand in both of ours and bowed low over it. What follows now may sound unscientific and irrational, but we all felt the same overwhelming sense of being in the presence of enormous power and sanctity so that, although I have a vivid mental picture of the next hour, I also remember it more as one does a dream than reality.

The *Ama Towa* was a youngish man, tall and graceful, with a gentle, almost effeminate, face and restless eyes. What I could see of his hair, under the turban, was long and black and it seemed likely that it was never cut, but tied up at the back in a queue. He had very strange large twisted lobes to his ears and rather bad teeth. On his left wrist he wore a simple black band and, on the fourth finger of his right hand, a ring containing a stone which looked like an opal.

As soon as he had sat down he took out a pretty wooden container with a long knife in it, in which he chopped up betel nuts before rolling them carefully in a leaf and putting them in his mouth to chew. His council, mostly older men with a dignity and confidence of elder statesmen, were also busy preparing betel, some with much finer containers made of wrought silver. Through the *jaksa* Christian Pelras began to ask questions to which the *Ama Towa* replied unhesitatingly, almost as though he knew what was going to be said before the words were spoken. His voice was high-pitched and impersonal, like that of a medium, and while he talked he moved restlessly, glancing about him and every now and then spitting a stream of red betel juice over the edge of the shelter. Christian explained that he was French, the doctor German, and we were English, and that we had come to ask him questions. The *Ama Towa* said that we were welcome and then asked if we came as official representatives of our respective governments or as private citizens. When told private citizens he asked if the Romans were still very large people. This required some explanation from Christian, who told us that for the Bugis Rome is Constantinople, arising from a confused legend that Alexander the Great came to Indonesia and is still referred to as Rajah Roma or Iskandar, a giant among men. We said that they were bigger than the Bugis, but not so huge—about the same size as the doctor who is a fairly tall man. Christian asked some more questions about the local names for parts of houses and certain plants and then, without warning, the *Ama Towa* turned to me and asked me why I had come, and what my particular purpose in Tana Towa was. I replied that I was interested in the power of *adat*, that in Europe and America there was not much *adat* any more and I had come to see how his people preserved theirs. He asked me if it was true that some Americans had been to the moon, and when I said it was, he answered that a people can only become strong if their *adat* is strong. Thereafter, no matter what their achievements, their society is sick if their *adat* becomes weak, and they will become like empty shells. The council members nodded at this and added their agreement.

He went on, '*Adat* is our mother; without it we are lost like orphans.'

I asked, 'How do you bring back *adat* to a people who have lost it?'

To which he answered, 'This is for the government to do. It's up to them to encourage *adat* and take the necessary steps to bring it back.'

I asked about materialism. 'How do you combat the desire, especially in the young, for new and exciting possessions? How can you prevent people wanting radios, bicycles and motor cars? How can the *adat* be strong if the people want change?'

In reply, he asked, 'Don't you have wise old men in Europe who tell the young what to do and how to behave?'

'Yes we do,' I answered, 'but no one listens to them any more.'

'If young people refuse to listen to the advice of their elders they are lost and should be punished. Here in Indonesia even high officials consult wise men and are told what is right. If what they plan is wrong they are influenced to think again.'

'Surely one's needs are created by the introduction of new gadgets, people are going to want more and more.'

'That is why we stick to our own *adat* here in Tana Towa so as not to allow the cycle to start.'

'But the cycle has started in Indonesia, and the people are encouraged to be modern and want more.'

'I cannot answer for Indonesia. I only know Tana Towa and here there is no problem and I am not afraid of the future. Here the *adat* is both the rule we follow and the message for the way ahead.'

What I found remarkable about the *Ama Towa*'s answers was not so much their content as the way they were uttered with complete conviction. In spite of the difficulties of expressing ideas through the medium of an interpreter, he seemed to understand exactly where my doubts and confusion lay, and to give his replies as simple, indisputable truths. I wanted to go further and ask him what would happen if the government implemented a plan, of which we had heard rumours, to turn the whole of Tana Towa into a giant tobacco plantation, involving the resettlement of its population. But the others felt that this would be going too far and, in fact, I found it hard to challenge such assurance and such total faith. As I noted in my diary at the time, it would have been like asking Jesus if he was having trouble attracting disciples. While this was going on he was smiling and looking straight at me; it suddenly occurred to me that I was incapable of meeting his eyes directly. Feeling that this was ridiculous, I made a conscious effort to do so, but was struck by such a sense of what I can only describe as 'presence', that I had to look away. The others admitted afterwards to having experienced the same sensations.

At the end, the *Ama Towa* turned to Doctor Meyer saying that he suffered from pains in his stomach. When he had described the symptoms, the doctor suggested that he probably had gastritis due to nervous tension and chewing too much betel. He promised to send some medicine from Makassar to the *jaksa,* who would see that it was delivered. At this, the audience was concluded, and the *Ama Towa* and his council filed off while we were invited to a nearby house for a meal. Inside, we saw how it was true that in Tana Towa nothing modern or manufactured was used. Over the fire hung some black iron pots, in which food was being prepared by a beautiful girl with red lips—not from betel or lipstick, but a locally produced dye. Everything else was made of wood or matting, except for the tooled brass trays on which tiny portions of rice, strange tasting, perhaps wild, vegetables and little chunks of excellent meat, were served. The trays had, I imagine, been introduced at some time, as had the only money they use which, we were told, consists exclusively of sixteenth century Portuguese coins, but we saw no plastic or tins, no paper or rubber, and even the wheel is forbidden. Everything was spotlessly clean and swept, inside and out, but it was the freedom from the sound of any motor or radio which contributed most to the sense of peace and tranquillity. We rode down a steep hill to see the original house which, as it had served as the prototype for all subsequent building, looked the same as all the others. Every bit of it had been faithfully replaced with fresh materials as they rotted over the years, but one of the uprights, made from the chili tree, had survived and was pointed out to us with pride. We passed the sacred forest which we were not allowed to enter. The *jaksa* said that there was a glade in the centre where no weeds grew, with a stone altar on which sacrifices were made.

All this had taken longer than we had realized, and it was dark an hour before we reached the noisy, hurly burly of Kalimpero again, stiff, sore and exhausted from the ride during which a thunderstorm had soaked us to the skin and lightning had flashed like a flaming sword expelling us from paradise.

PART FOUR

The Moluccas

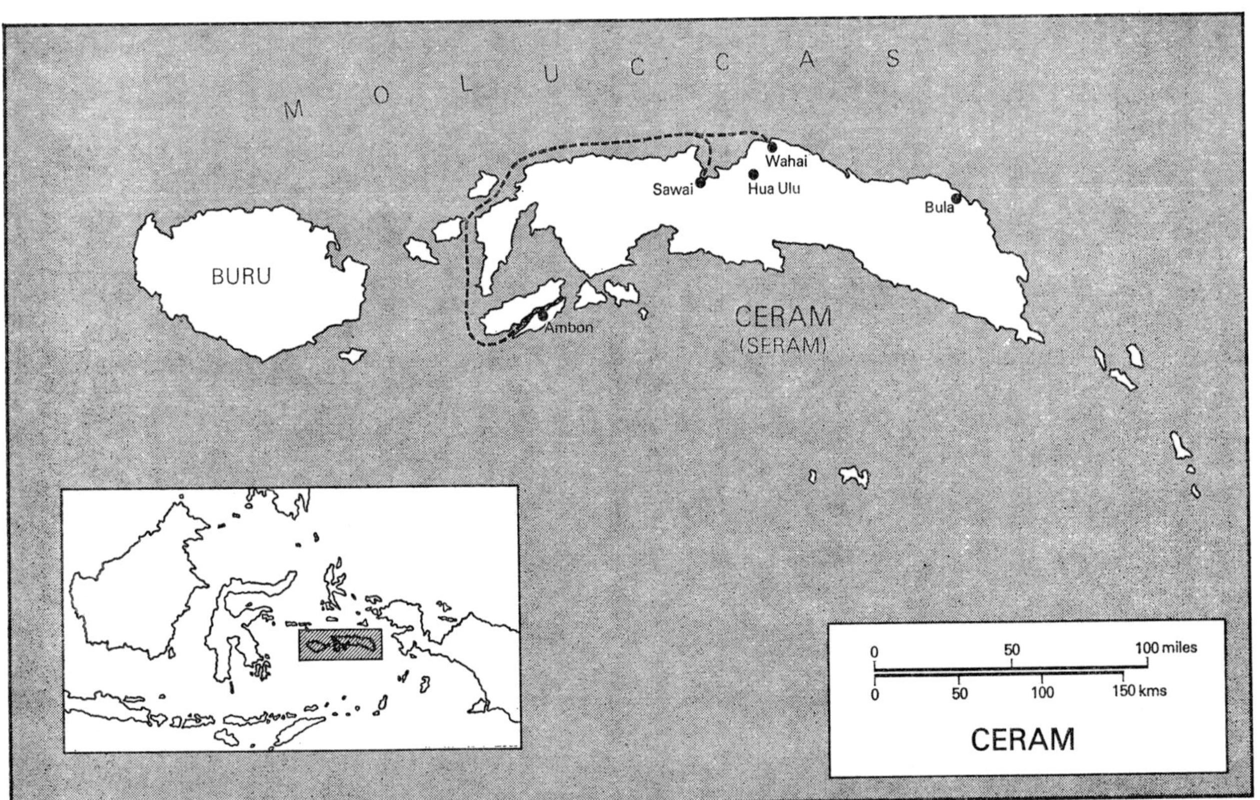
MOLUCCAS
BURU
Sawai
Wahai
Hua Ulu
Bula
Ambon
CERAM
(SERAM)
0
50
100 miles
0
50
100
150 kms
CERAM

Ceram

THE Moluccas, the legendary 'spice islands', long sought by European traders in the Middle Ages, lie between Celebes and New Guinea. There, Alfred Russel Wallace developed his theory of evolution during his travels round the island from 1854 to 1862. While suffering from a fever in 1858, the concept of the survival of the fittest came to him in a flash, inspiring him to write to Darwin and so spur him into publishing *Origin of Species*, which had been written nineteen years previously. Wallace's own book, *Malaysian Archipelago*, recently reissued by Dover Publications, New York, gives an excellent picture of the plant, animal and insect life of the islands. Reading it later on my return to England was a profoundly humbling experience. The intellectual giants of the nineteenth century, with their capacity to encompass all the known sciences of their time and to travel for years at a stretch through virtually unknown regions, noting everything they saw and laying the foundations of classifications and theories which still largely hold good today, can only fill one with awe. The narrow belt between Borneo and Celebes, representing a sharp division between indigenous species—those of Asia to the west and Australia to the east—is still known as 'Wallace's Line'. With increasing specialization no scientist can now have the same depth of vision, with the result that, as problems concerning the environment become more acute, comprehensive solutions become harder to grasp. I also found it interesting reading Wallace to realize that over one hundred years ago, at a time when the Dutch administration was firmly in control providing an exclusive infrastructure for the European traveller, expeditions were, in certain respects, easier to equip and organize than they are now, once one moves outside the centres served by the airline system.

The whole timescale was, of course, vastly extended. Wallace spent eight years travelling about fourteen thousand miles through the archipelago and making sixty or seventy separate journeys, each, as he says, 'involving some preparation and loss of time'. A great deal of the time must have been taken up with the slow voyages between the islands, the necessity for which is now removed by the network of internal flights. However, once on the spot, Wallace met a succession of helpful officials who thought nothing of providing sophisticated hospitality for days on end, transport and bearers. On the journey to Ambon he describes enjoying 'a voyage more than I had ever done before'. This was on a 'roomy and comfortable vessel, although it would only go six miles an hour in the finest weather'.

> There are no cabin servants, as every cabin passenger invariably brings his own, and the ship's stewards attend only to the saloon and the eating department. At six a.m. a cup of tea or coffee is provided for those who like it. At seven to eight there is a light breakfast of tea, eggs, sardines, etc. At ten, Madeira, gin, and bitters are brought on deck as a whet for a substantial eleven o'clock breakfast, which differs from a dinner only in the absence of soup. Cups of tea and coffee are brought round at three p.m.; bitters, etc, again at five; a good dinner with beer and claret at half-past six, concluded by tea and coffee at eight. Between whiles, beer and soda water are supplied when called for, so there is no lack of little gastronomical excitements to while away the tedium of a sea voyage.

On Ceram itself he received a boat 'rather larger than necessary with a crew of twenty men'. When he made sorties into the interior he 'put up the smallest quantity of baggage possible for a six days' trip ... with six men carrying my baggage and their own provisions, and a lad from Awaiya, who was accustomed to catch butterflies for me'. This is not to say that he did not endure great hardship and privation, but only to illustrate that there were then certain compensations for the speed with which journeys can be undertaken today.

We flew from Makassar across the two southern arms of Celebes, sparsely forested and populated by scattered farming communities; over the wide Banda sea to the east where coral reefs were visible through the blue water, but seldom broke the surface; on past the rugged, dark green island of Buru where seventeen thousand Communists and suspected sympathizers have been interned since the 1965 coup, a politically sensitive place so that access by anthropologists to the rich tribal cultures of the unexplored interior is at present forbidden; and then, after a tantalizing glimpse of the huge rainswept island of Ceram to the north, where mountains towered to nine thousand feet, we landed at the airport for Ambon, the provincial capital of the Moluccas. The islands are famous for their bird life, and the first sight that greeted us as we stepped out onto the runway was a stack of cages full of parrots and cockatoos. I am not sure what the international regulations are for the transportation of birds, but these looked utterly wretched, squashed three or four deep and baked in the sun. While waiting for our baggage to be cleared, we counted the inmates. Scarlet and green parrots the size of pigeons, segregated according to colour, were packed one hundred to a cage measuring four feet by two feet by eight inches, and already many of those on the lower layers were dead. Underneath, were larger, white cockatoos, but managing to look so miserable that we were tempted for a moment to be like Saint Francis and spend the rest of our money buying the lot and setting them free. Guiltily deciding that it was none of our business we climbed into one of the three waiting mini buses, where we, in turn, were joined by so many others that we were given a taste of how the parrots must have felt. The drive around the long thin bay to the town of Ambon followed a narrow road along the seashore, bridging a series of clear streams from which gaily dressed washerwomen and children bathing waved to us. The people, now of mixed Malay-Papuan descent, were noticeably darker than in the rest of Indonesia, and the scene with neat little houses and gardens growing sugar cane, pineapples and brightly coloured flowers under waving coconut palms, reminded us of the north coast of Jamaica, where my brother lives. In the town, hoping it would be like the seedy but romantic *Grand Hotel* in Makassar, with its atmosphere of a Somerset Maugham short story, we checked into the old colonial *Anggrek* (orchid) *Hotel*. This was a grave mistake at eight pounds per night with inedible food, dust inches thick, a stuffy unventilated cell of a bedroom and a bar containing not one single bottle of anything.

However, as soon as we made contact with Father Rutges, our spirits rose as must have those of all fortunate enough to meet this splendid old Dutch priest, who has lived in the Moluccas for forty years, and probably knows the area in general, and Ambon in particular, better than anyone else. I had written to him from England on the recommendation of a mutual friend, and had received an enthusiastic reply saying, 'Welcome to these faraway islands!', but he had also warned me not to expect that I would be able to achieve anything in a short time: 'The biggest problem here has always been TRANSPORTATION, how do I go to there, and how do I come back from there.... Don't make any time schedule and take with you the most needed "patience"; the only certainty here is the horrible "*Barangkali*" i.e. maybe, perhaps.' Through him I hoped to contact an Italian anthropologist, Valerio Valeri, working with a remote tribe on Ceram, but I was not very hopeful about our chances of reaching him. Father Rutges gave us the incredible news that Valeri's wife, Renée, was actually in Ambon and returning by boat to join her husband in a day or two. While the Father took us to the Governor, the Chief of Police and the

Department of Immigration, securing letters of authority on our behalf and opening doors which we might never have penetrated by our own efforts, we made friends with Renée. She was a charming, red-haired Swedish girl, who spoke excellent English and expressed delight at having company on the journey. We were to travel on the *Huni Moki V*, a small tramp steamer which would drop us on the north coast of Ceram at the nearest point on the shore to the inland village of the Hua Ulu people with whom the Valeris were living for two years. If our amazing luck held it would collect us on its return from Bula further along the coast and return us to Ambon. Since there are often intervals of two or three months between such sailings, it all seemed too good to be true.

Father Rutges was the sole Catholic priest to have survived the Japanese occupation of the Moluccas. His bishop and twelve other priests had been lined up on the beach and shot, but he was away at the time on one of the outer islands and had then spent the rest of the war suffering appalling degradations in a prison camp. Now, he was building a much needed leper hospital outside the town and, with boundless energy, showed us the plans he had drawn himself, and took us out to see how work was progressing on the site. In marked contrast to so many of the depressing half-completed projects we had seen in Indonesia, where large sums of money, often provided by international aid, had mysteriously vanished, causing work to be abandoned, here was a worthwhile, well planned operation which was clearly going to succeed. Due to the determination and drive of its progenitor, the money was being raised and not a penny was being wasted or embezzled. It was hard, in view of the glaring need in Ambon for hospitals, sanitation and public works, not to draw an unfavourable comparison with the extravagant sports complex on the hill above the town where an olympic swimming pool, badminton courts and a huge auditorium, had been erected for the use of the military garrison. I promised, as the least I could do in return for his kindness, to urge Oxfam to support Father Rutges's hospital, and later did so.

The *Huni Moki V* sailed on the ebb tide at two in the morning. Fortified with several brandies at a bar in the harbour, tranquillized with Librium against sea sickness, for the waters around Ceram are notorious, and full of aspirins as we had all picked up nasty colds in Ambon, we rolled aboard, oblivious of the smell of rotting fish and diesel fumes. The crew of six caught fish from the stern and boiled them over an open fire before mixing them with rice and sharing them out with us and the handful of other passengers who all slept on the open deck. We were allowed to squeeze into the narrow wheelhouse where we could see over the head of the old Chinese skipper as he guided the ship through the treacherous reefs around the coast, steering at night through a wall of blackness and often rain without benefit of any navigational aid except for an old compass. A lot of these boats do sink from being overloaded in a storm, or through hitting rocks, and when they do the crew and passengers are usually all drowned. The only lifeboat was a single dugout canoe lashed to the side.

The coast of Ceram is lined with sandy beaches and occasional palm groves behind which the dark green forested hills rise up to the mountains of the interior, the highest peak being Binaija at just over three thousand metres (9 905 feet).

We reached Sawai at dawn, a gem of a village nestling under a cliff, with the wooden houses built out onto the sea on stilts. Every house was palm thatched—no corrugated iron here yet—and a pretty white mosque stood in the central square. We went ashore and had tea at the only shop, which sold bolts of cloth and fish hooks, and then went for a swim in the Sawai river, navigable for its total length of two hundred metres. Sweet fresh water gushes out of the base of the cliff into a wide shoulder deep pool with a hard stone floor and flat rocks all around, an ideal place for the washing of clothes and of people as the suds and dirt float quickly out to sea down the short canal through the village. The novel—indeed never-before-witnessed—sight of three fair-haired and very pink bodies, soaping and enjoying themselves in the pool, attracted the entire population to watch and comment in amazed delight.

A canoe with sails and outriggers was arranged to take us out of the bay and along the coast to a place from which we would walk to the Hua Ulu. Efforts were made to dissuade us. 'They will eat you,' they said. There was no wind to fill the sail, and the two boys from the village paddled in slow motion making one leisurely stroke to two or three of mine. After four hours we had barely rounded the headland and I found it much quicker, when the beach began again, to get out and tow it along, while the two girls, like Edwardian society ladies, lay back under an unlikely multicoloured umbrella belonging to Renée. It was a hot airless day and the sea and sand shimmered invitingly. I felt foolish expending so much energy in such idyllic surroundings, but, at the same time, I was worried that if we were not back waiting on the shore when the *Huni Moki V*, now steaming over the horizon to the east, returned we might be forced to spend a month or more enjoying them. At last we reached the huts where two Hua Ulu families, who had settled on the coast, were living. But the men whom, we hoped, would guide us up into the mountains, were away cutting sago, and so we went further on to the mouth of a river where the local 'policeman' lived. Since the troubles, when Ambon had attempted to secede from the nation, Ceram has been under military rule. This official, wielding virtually total power, was said to exploit the local tribe, insisting that they wear sarongs rather than bark loin cloths and then forcing them to barter exorbitant quantities of parrots and cockatoos for cheap material which he supplied. Perhaps some of the unfortunate birds we had seen at the airport had come from here. Luckily he was away, but his wife and family were friendly and welcoming, insisting that we spend the night with them. As Renée was still suffering badly from 'Ambon 'flu', and the predictable heavy afternoon rain was about to begin, this was probably just as well. Renée's descriptions of the Hua Ulu were becoming more and more glowing as we neared them and we longed to reach their village, but walking through a tropical downpour was something to be avoided, as was committing ourselves to an uncomfortable wet night in the jungle en route. When the rain cleared in the evening we were able to walk along the beach, and watch the sunset while thousands of crabs scuttled in and out of the waves, or raced for the shelter of the undergrowth as we passed.

Three Hua Ulu men arrived the next morning to show us the way and help carry the supplies Renée had collected in Ambon; our equipment, weighing about twenty kilos, was packed in my knapsack and Marika had a small holdall and the camera case. The policeman's family would have been offended had we offered to pay, but Renée, who had stayed there before, had established a system whereby she bought some rice from them and, not questioning the asking price, paid about double its value. This satisfied everybody's honour. The two elder Hua Ulu were married men which entitled them to wear red turbans. Their skins were much darker than those of the Mentawaians and Dayaks, and they both had bushy black moustaches beneath slightly flattened noses. Under their turbans they had long hair, tightly coiled in two neat buns, and we were immediately struck by the strength and alertness of their faces and the lithe easy way they moved. This could have been due to Renée's build up, but I don't think so as I remember being quite prepared to find that she had exaggerated when describing them. The eldest was called Tikele, a silent man and one of the handful of Hua Ulu who had voluntarily chosen to live on the coast away from the rest of the tribe. Kuweiamani, who was younger, had recently eloped with a girl from another tribe. This had caused problems as they now wanted a Hua Ulu girl in exchange, and these were in short supply; also none had any desire to go and live with a strange people whom they despised. As a result, he and his wife were lying low with Tikele until the fuss died down. He was an ugly man with a severe squint, but a highly intelligent and entertaining character. The third Hua Ulu, Hari, was unmarried and he simply wore a strip of bamboo around his head with his copious, rather frizzy, hair fluffed out under it like an Afro haircut.

After retracing our steps along the beach for a mile or so, we turned inland and, for two hours, walked through a fetid swamp sometimes on logs or tree-trunks—by now Marika was getting much better at not falling off—and sometimes up to our waists in oozing black mud. Then we began to climb through clean primary jungle where the going was much easier with a clear path and almost bare ground under the tall trees. It was pleasantly cool too, with few insects, a relief after the swamps where the mosquitoes had been fairly active. We walked fast now through the silence and the stillness, enjoying the feeling of being in an enchanted forest. The path became gradually steeper, following the bed of a stream and passing through rocks overgrown with vegetation, until we reached the crest of a range of hills marking the half way point. Here, we stopped and rested. Bird life was plentiful now, in particular flocks of large black hornbills with brightly coloured beaks. They were about the size of geese and took off from the trees above us with a great flapping and crashing, the air vibrating in their feathers like swans taking off from water. There were also large numbers of crimson parrots and noisy white cockatoos, shrieking hysterically to warn each other of our approach; also a small iridescent blue bird, the size of a humming bird, which came and perched quite tamely on a flower a yard from my hand. We saw several varieties of butterfly, some large green and yellow Birdwings and ghostly blue ones flitting in and out of the shadows which reminded me of the Morphos of South America, but were probably a variety called *Papilio Ulysses Ulysses* only found on Ceram. There was also a particularly beautiful blue and white one with a pattern on its wings just like Batik, the famous Javanese material. But there are no monkeys in Ceram, almost the only indigenous mammal being the *cus-cus*, and that is a marsupial as Ceram is more Australian than Asian. Deer are also common, having been introduced by the Dutch, and so are wild pigs, but they, too, were probably introduced by man at some time in the distant past.

The torrential daily rains began at midday, soaking through everything in seconds and making the prospect of arrival at the village even more enticing. At last, as the rains eased, we came in sight of it, far across a valley on the side of a hill surrounded by mountains. One more river lay between us and this was in flood deeper, Renée said, than she had ever seen it. There was no way of carrying the baggage across, and so we sat on the bank and waited. After a while, since the level showed no sign of dropping, Hari and I left our loads behind and, armed with long poles, jumped in. The water was warmer than the rain, but the current was too strong to fight against and we were soon out of our depth. Swimming hard, Hari using a very effective dog paddle while I did my usual, rather ragged, crawl until I ran out of breath and resorted to the breast stroke, we reached the far bank half a mile downstream. Shaking ourselves like dogs, we raced each other up the hill towards the village. As we came over the rise Hari rushed off and I found myself walking alone up the wide open space between the houses. This was an exciting and marvellous moment which I savoured by walking slowly. I also needed to get my breath back. Apart from the Valeris I was the first European ever to set foot in the Hua Ulu village. No missionaries have been allowed there, and they have sworn that they will take the head of the first one who tries to convert them. They do still take heads from time to time and it suddenly occurred to me that I might be providing them with just the opportunity they had been waiting for. However, Renée had said that their house was at the far end of the village, and so I walked stolidly towards it while the Hua Ulu came out of their houses to watch. I must have looked a strange sight to Valerio, the first white man, albeit a very bedraggled and wet one, that he had seen for eighteen months. I saw him standing out on the gallery of his house, a tall and very emaciated man with a black beard and spectacles. Renée and Marika had encouraged me to play a trick on him, pretending that I had just wandered in on my own by chance and, to be even more cruel, by saying that there had been no sign of Renée in Ambon, only rumours of an outbreak of headhunting near the coast. But when it came to the point, I hadn't the heart and simply introduced myself and put him in the picture. He quickly collected some rope and we returned through the village, this time stopping to explain who I was. I urged him to emphasize that we were not missionaries, and only planned to stay for a couple of days.

By the time we reached the river again the water had dropped a couple of feet, and we able to swim the stores across at some shallows further downstream. There was a fire burning in a small hut by the bank and we huddled round this to dry ourselves. Valerio handed round betel, which he chews constantly when not smoking his pipe. It had wrought havoc with his teeth which looked the same as most of the Hua Ulu's, blackened and with some missing. The betel mixture tasted much better than any I had had before, consisting of the nut with a special local root and some lime ground together into a wad. It was much less bitter than when wrapped in a leaf. We all felt in a holiday mood at having arrived safely. Renée was glad to be home and, once we had climbed up the hill again, we were delighted by the house which the Hua Ulu had built for the Valeris, and which I now had a chance to see over properly. On stilts and open along one side it was like a miniature longhouse and, in fact, many of the tribes of Ceram used to live in longhouses before the Dutch forbade it and burnt them all. The kitchen and sleeping area were walled in, while the gallery had a raised platform at either end with a fire built on a stone slab where we sat and talked looking out at the magnificent view over the village to the hills beyond, with the mist rising off them and the sun setting behind the wall of mountains in the distance. I could imagine no more idyllic place for an anthropologist to do his field work. While Valerio and I discussed their future, and the future of all such tribal peoples, the Hua Ulu quietly came and went, shyly inspecting Marika and me, accepting cigarettes and, from time to time, joining in the conversation. We had a warm feeling of being quite welcome, and it was clear that the Valeris had been fully accepted into the community. Valerio was pessimistic, seeing many insoluble paradoxes surrounding the problem. In the first place, the western world, so concerned now to protect nature, has itself destroyed its own environment and so lives in an artificial state. If we really believed in our ecological ideals we would have to try and return to a pre-agricultural hunter gatherer way of life, which is clearly impossible. Meanwhile, the Hua Ulu, who virtually do still live in the Stone Age, have a quite different concept of nature, and they certainly don't respect it. In fact, said Valerio, they fight it all the way. How can one hope to reconcile these two attitudes?

Another paradox lies in the fact that the Hua Ulu want to remain where they are and to live according to their present lifestyle; but at the same time they want the benefits of western technology. In their particular case, however, he felt that this might be a happy paradox, since their isolation is not only physical but also a state of mind. They are passionately desirous of remaining true to their culture, observing their *adat*, worshipping their ancestors, following their ritual and continuing to be Hua Ulu and animist. This need not necessarily conflict with the adoption of new techniques. For instance, in the medical field, unlike many other peoples in Indonesia, they see a clear distinction between physical and psychological illness. They, themselves, in their own medicine, recognize the difference between practical steps such as chewing curative roots and applying plants to wounds, on the one hand, and placating spirits, calling back souls which have wandered off, and calming emotional disturbances, on the other. A sensitive doctor, willing to help rather than effect a complete change, would certainly be a great asset to them, even if he could only visit them two or three times a year. The main problem facing the Hua Ulu, and one which they long to solve but have no cure for, is a rapidly declining birth rate which is reaching a stage where there is a real possibility of extinction. This may be genetic or there may be some quite simple physical or dietary explanation, but Valerio was convinced that it was not psychological as with some of the indian tribes in Brazil who want to die out because life has become unbearable. The Hua Ulu, on the contrary, are proud and confident about their future, and only want more children so as to make themselves even stronger as a tribe. There are now about one hundred and fifty Hua Ulu, of which one hundred and thirty-three live in the village while the remainder live nearby or on the coast. When Valerio first arrived there were one hundred and thirty-nine, but since then eight old people have died and only three children had been born, one of which also later died.

According to Valerio the total population of Ceram is about one hundred thousand and, as it was estimated at nearly seventy thousand in 1910, there has been no great population explosion. In west Ceram, and on the south coast, there has been some settlement, but in central Ceram there has been a marked decrease. Some of the depopulation has been caused by epidemics, while forced conversion to Christianity, by Protestant missionaries from Ambon, has caused paranoid schizophrenia in the people making them discouraged and confused so that they are afraid of having offended the spirits of their ancestors without being able, really, to believe in the effectiveness of what they have been converted to. As a result, many groups stopped having children. Also during the twenty-three years of uninterrupted war, which raged over Ceram, many members of the inland tribes were killed. First there was the Japanese occupation and subsequent liberation by allied forces; then there was civil war which continued until 1963 when Muslim rebels, Christians fighting for an independent south Molucca state, and government forces, all used people from the rural villages of whom many died. Valerio felt that, in any case, the numbers of Hua Ulu had probably dropped below the level at which they could survive as a distinct tribe. 'The story of primitive man is a history of constantly disappearing societies. They either gradually die out when their numbers become too few to provide the necessary replacements, or they are forced to merge with their neighbours. A surprising byproduct of this on Ceram, where the process has certainly been taking place for some time, is the way in which aspects of the various cultures have been diffused. For instance, you sometimes find the same song sung in half a dozen different languages even though the people are enemies.' Although doubtful about the Hua Ulu's chances of survival as a cultural identity, he maintained strongly that fusion into the coastal society would represent an actual lowering of their standard of living. 'The people there are selfconsciously aware of being poor, and try without sufficient resources to copy a "modern" way of life, so becoming dependent on imported foods and materials which are difficult and expensive to acquire. As a result, the food they eat is of lower nutritional value, and the way they cook it spoils the taste. Here, the main cooking utensil is the hollow bamboo tube in which the vitamins are retained and the food value is enhanced.' While entirely agreeing with him in principle, we had not had the Valeris' opportunity to accustom ourselves to Hua Ulu taste, and struggled manfully to enjoy the ancient maggoty pork, kindly brought to us that first evening, the putrefying smell of which still lingers in my mind six months later.

Among all the tribes of central Ceram the taking of a head used to be the inseparable core of all ceremonies. Most have now been forced to abandon the practice and the Hua

Ulu know well that there would be trouble if they were caught at it. They dare not play their flutes any more because the music would attract their ancestors, who would be angry if they arrived and found no head had been prepared and that the ritual was not being properly observed. When an accidental death occurs among them, for example after a man has had a fatal fall from a tree, the village must be abandoned and, for a time, they scatter, living a nomadic life, then they come together again to build a new village and every village must have a *baileu* or clan house. The Hua Ulu had moved to their present site only four years before and the *baileu* had been built with full attendant ceremony a year later. Valerio said it was unthinkable that this could have been done without a human head being placed under the central pillar. On most other occasions, however, a small part of the head, such as some hair, blood or teeth, has to suffice. This must come from someone killed by a member of the tribe, but it makes it easier to escape detection if the whole head is not removed and the killing takes place a long way from the village. Quite recently, the Noa Ulu, a related tribe living near the south coast, had built a new *baileu*. They were supposed to have abandoned headhunting completely, but around this time three Philippinos, from a lumber camp, had disappeared and the Hua Ulu, hearing of it, had nodded wisely drawing their own conclusions.

In the old days, when headhunting was the norm, every adult in a tribe represented at least three heads taken. When a child was to be born the mother went to the menstruation hut for the birth, and according to tribal custom, could not leave it until a head had been obtained. Similarly, one was required for the initiation ceremony of each boy and girl and for each marriage. To become a great chief, a man had to take at least ten heads and many took more. This produced, what Valerio called, 'the impossible equation', for how could there be enough heads to go round if everyone followed the same custom? The only possible answer had to be that it was at a time of constant migration from the overpopulated north Moluccas, with successive waves of settlers supplying the necessary constant supplement.

Headhunting has been worldwide. It was certainly practised by many Stone Age peoples in Europe and survived among the Montenegrans until this century where heads were still occasionally taken during the Balkan war of 1912–13. In the British Isles it was known among the Irish and Scottish in the Middle Ages and traces of the tradition linger on in the killing of a pig and sprinkling of its blood on the fields in the autumn to ensure a good crop next spring. Sometimes associated with cannibalism, the practice is normally based on a belief that the life force of the victim resides in the head and is something concrete which can be transferred to the new owner. This belief seems to have arisen spontaneously in many widely scattered cultures and to represent a very deep-seated part of human nature. While it is understandable that it should have been among the first objects of colonists and missionaries to stamp it out, viewing it as abhorrent paganism, it is at the same time a pity that, as a result, few researchers have had the opportunity of examining the wider implications of headhunting in depth and assessing its rôle as a component of a tribe's culture. Valerio was therefore in a rare position to gather information on the subject and produce original material, research which could lead to a better understanding of the needs of the many other tribes now settled nearer the coast.

We walked around the village admiring the carvings on the houses, and calling in to sit and talk with the various chiefs. This is a popular Hua Ulu pastime, and they use the same word for visiting as for playing. There are several chiefs, each fulfilling a different rôle. The 'land' chief was a very old man whose job it was to settle disputes over where each family should plant their crops, and who had first claim to each wild fruit tree growing in the surrounding jungle. The 'ceremonial' chief, perhaps the one most hit by the prohibition of headhunting, was responsible, among other things, for organizing the different dances which are many and varied. The most exciting is the *chakalele*, or war dance, but this is seldom done now and is best avoided by outsiders as they tend to get carried away. The 'government' chief is the most important, being elected unlike the others, and it is he alone who undertakes all negotiations with the outside world. They have had little trouble from the authorities so far, although a few years ago a policeman did arrive and tell them to give up their dances and wear proper clothes. The ceremonial chief cut his throat, but was prevented by the others from removing his head so that he later recovered and was sent back to the coast. Although worried by the possibility of repercussions at the time, they said it had proved a very effective way of discouraging any further calls by the police. There had only been one other visit from the authorities since then, which had resulted from a rumour started in Ambon that the Valeris had had their heads taken. The Bupati from Wahai had come to see that they were all right and had made a speech to the assembled Hua Ulu, which Valerio had had to translate as few of them speak any Indonesian. Surprisingly, the Bupati had said that they were perfectly entitled to practise their own culture and that they should not listen to missionaries and others who might come and tell them that they had to change their ways. This was an unusually enlightened attitude however, and conflicts with official policy which, as part of the national plan to integrate the diverse peoples of the islands, encourages inland societies such as the Hua Ulu to move to the coast and plant coconuts. Although understandable as policy from an administrative point of view in a country as widespread and loosely united as Indonesia, its wisdom in relation to Ceram is questionable. Copra, the end product of such an economy, is a rapidly declining and unstable market on which to be dependent, and depopulating the vast interior of the people who best understand it and could help to release its undoubted potential, must be wasteful from an economic aspect.

The Hua Ulu say that they will never allow themselves to be converted to either Christianity or Islam, they say this with great determination adding that if conversion is forced on them they will kill themselves, men, women and children, rather than submit. They also refuse to send most of their children away to school. As a compromise they have agreed to allow three to go to the school at Opit, near Sawai, but two of these come from the family of Tikele who already lives by the sea. They consider that educating their children themselves in familiar surroundings, and according to their own traditions, is more important. I felt that they would find no fault with the argument that, while headhunting may be out, there is a lot more to being a Hua Ulu than that, and there is much to be said for growing up in the security of a known environment.

Every house is decorated with carvings of a high quality no longer produced elsewhere in Ceram. Many of the young boys display a natural talent which their elders encourage them to practise, learning the complex traditional spiral and geometric designs as well as how to reproduce lifelike animals. For the uprights supporting the houses a species of giant fern, also known in Africa, is used. The wood is most suitable for being worked, and they often display surprising contrasts, bas-reliefs of realistic crocodiles, pigs' heads, lizards and birds interspersed with surrealist impressions of great beauty and charm. The *baileu* has the best carvings around its base, above which rises a really magnificent spacious hall with a wide wooden dance floor under the sweeping tightly interwoven roof, which reaches down almost to the level of the platform. The men, in their red turbans and bark loin cloths, the women in colourful sarongs, and the polite respectful children, deeply interested in the presence of strangers, but never shouting or following, all seemed to us to compose a perfect picture of integrated harmony.

A remarkable feature of the Hua Ulu is their ability to speak several different languages. For some reason these have proliferated and there are said to be thirty-five distinct and mutually unintelligible dialects on the island, apart from Indonesian and Chinese. They sing a lot, remembering songs running to literally thousands of verses. Valerio said that often, after spending an hour or more recounting a myth to him, they would begin once more and sing it again six or seven times, each time in a new language. The village had a wonderfully peaceful secure feeling; the people were generous, kind and polite, wandering in and out of the Valeris' house with presents of pigmeat, bananas, coconuts, sago or crayfish. Throughout the day they came and sat on the gallery to talk or just to watch whatever might be going on; they examined each article which Renée had brought back from Ambon, in particular a pair of baseball boots she had bought for Valerio, remembering how often he had cut his feet, and similar to the ones we wore and swore by. He rejected them, however, saying he preferred to go barefoot like the Hua Ulu. He had reached the village originally the hard way, walking for ten days across the island with a heavy load and, although his feet had suffered without shoes, he intended to leave the same way, rightly believing that if you can take it, and once your soles have hardened, it is much easier to remain upright on the wet slippery paths without shoes. Sometimes, as they watched us talking, one of the men would play a few notes on a long thin violin with a gourd at the end as soundbox; often they sang, especially in the early morning when we could hear singing wafted up to us from almost every house in the village. Even the children, when they were unhappy, sang a mournful song rather than crying as other children do. Meanwhile, in spite of the leisurely relaxed air of life being an enjoyable and interesting affair, everyone was busy making things; beautiful baskets were made from sago bark, waterproof containers for betel nut and tobacco; larger rattan baskets for carrying produce collected in the forest; bows and arrows for hunting, tipped with bone, bamboo or sometimes a sliver of metal, and long throwing spears for hunting deer. They also make very effective traps for catching wild pig which, they said, were plentiful. We saw a *cus-cus* being prepared for cooking, small and naked when skinned with rather horrifyingly human hands and feet but excellent meat. Chickens run around in the village, but they are sacred and not eaten, going off into the bushes to lay their eggs and contributing little to the economy.

A stream ran past the village, diverted here and there into bamboo pipes, which brought running water right up to some of the houses. Later, on the coast, the Muslim settlers asked us repeatedly how we could tolerate being with the Hua Ulu. 'They are ignorant, dangerous people who never wash,' they said. When we replied that they washed several times a day adding, when stung to anger by their prejudice, 'More often than you do!', we were met with blank incredulity. At the same time, they found it confusing, and rather upsetting, that an Italian 'professor' should prefer to go and live in such squalor to the obvious civilization of their community. The division between the coastal Malays and the interior tribesmen which is such a feature of the outer islands of Indonesia is never as clearcut as it appears. They are distinguished less by race than by the influence of Islam spread by the Arab, Indian and Malay traders who visited the shores of the islands through the centuries but seldom penetrated far into the interior. One of the reasons for this was the absence of much other protein than pork, forbidden them by the tenets of their religion. Therefore, although the indigenous tribesmen have largely moved to the coast and adopted the superficial life style of the coastal society with its dependence on fishing, maritime trade and the cultivation of coconut palms, they are nonetheless living in an alien culture and cling to many of their old beliefs and customs. A valuable contribution could be made to the stability and prosperity of their communities by studying their origins and needs so that they do not become disorientated through their lack of a secure cultural base.

* * *

While Valerio was very concerned about the difficulties facing his tribe, and anxious to help them, he expressed a doubt that in the long run there was much that he could do. As an anthropologist he found himself in a familiar dilemma. It is a discipline beset by conflicting pressures and loyalties, making it hard to achieve all that most of its adherents would wish. In the first place, there is the problem of finding the money to finance field work, and the necessary long distance travel associated with it. Then there is the question of time, involving long periods away from home and family with all the resulting domestic upheavals and, for a married man, the responsibilities of a wife and children. Often, considerable hardship and sacrifice must be endured, aggravated by the knowledge that your contemporaries, remaining close to the sources of power, are either feathering their academic nests or opting to make their fortunes in the world of business. Certainly, stuck in a lonely and isolated corner of the world it is easy to start imagining that everyone else has the opportunity to prepare a comfortable and secure future for themselves, while you, yourself, have been forgotten. Meanwhile, a close personal involvement develops with the people under study. If they are going to reveal the secrets of their culture and beliefs you must foster an intimate relationship with them, out of which mutual trust can grow. Inevitably, during this process, you will begin to care about what happens to them; you will become angry at abuses perpetrated against them, whether by greedy land speculators, by missionaries of rival sects competing for their souls, or misguided officials wishing to change their ways so as to make them easier to administer. Through living with them you will see how these forces, however well intentioned, are often not in their best interest. You will want to help them by speaking out, by writing articles, agitating on their behalf and by publicizing their plight to the outside world, where you are able to travel and they are not.

But, at the same time, you want to return to them; because by understanding and learning more about them you can help them; because this alone is the area in which you are the expert, they are your speciality and it may be important to your career to build on this; also, perhaps, because you have grown to love them and are reluctant to lose touch. However, if you say too much, criticizing their government directly or by implication, you will certainly not be allowed to come back. Indeed, you may well do more harm than good, stirring up trouble by drawing attention to them when they might otherwise have been left in peace.

Anthropologists traditionally see themselves as scientists, who should study their subject dispassionately, serving a useful purpose simply through the collection of facts which may be correlated with others gathered elsewhere, producing theories and patterns which contribute to the general fund of human knowledge. Valerio felt that, in a way, he could be most useful to the Hua Ulu by providing them with moral support, demonstrating through his presence and interest that their lives were valid and worthy of respect. This was particularly necessary in their case where all around believed them to be stupid and inferior. While I can sympathize with his point of view and have, indeed, heard it expressed by many anthropologists in the field, I do not feel that it goes far enough. The argument can too easily be turned around so that the researcher ends up accused of exploiting the people himself, using them as guinea pigs for his own academic ends. An intellectually courageous anthropologist, such as I believe Valerio to be, should be able to study his subject in depth while, at the same time, involving himself in their problems and their future, becoming their ambassador and advocate in a world which so often threatens their survival. A growing number of younger anthropologists subscribe to this view, supported, as is so often the case in human affairs, by those elder statesmen whose reputations and authority are unchallenged. Naturally, tact is required, as well as sympathy for the national government. Often hardly aware of the existence of such an insignificant minority within its boundaries, and always beset by far more pressing affairs of state, they may be surprised and even offended that concern should be expressed for people who represent the opposite of all their progressive national ideals. But it is with them that the ultimate authority rests to respect the rights of all their citizens and, as the example of Brazil has shown, a little pressure can sometimes produce vehement protestations of willingness to do so. As lessons are learned about the dangers of rapid change and ill-conceived tampering with fragile ecosystems, as the energy crisis grows and the raw materials necessary for an expanding industrial society shrink, it may even be that we will go cap in hand to seek the remaining 'primitive' societies and ask their advice. It will be ironic if when we do so we find that they no longer exist.

We walked back to the coast, wading the now shallow river with ease, and then hurrying to avoid being caught by the afternoon rain. Our feet had developed painful sores which showed signs of becoming septic, so that it was an intense pleasure to reach the seashore again, remove our canvas shoes and walk barefoot in the sand. We were relieved to hear that the *Huni Moki V* had not been seen to pass again. After a night with the policeman's family, we hitched a lift eastwards on a passing canoe to the little town of Wahai where, miraculously, we arrived at the same time as the little steamer, coming from the opposite direction, tied up on its return journey. We were once more given our berth in the wheelhouse before setting sail again for Ambon, stopping at Sawai and some other settlements on the coast to collect cargo. At one of the villages, where the palm-fringed beach and thatched houses fulfilled all the requirements of a travel poster advertising the balmy South Seas, we swam ashore to the delight of a hundred children who thought we were quite the funniest things they had ever seen. Cheering enthusiastically, they accompanied us as we walked along the shore collecting seashells and, when we returned to lie and sunbathe on deck, our every move produced a concerted, and in time predictable, response. This reached ridiculous lengths when, as though conducting an orchestra, we were able by merely lifting a foot in one direction, or waving a hand in the other, to produce a screamed response from different sections of the beach. The final deafening chorus, when we rose to wave goodbye, gave us an inkling of how dictators on their balconies must feel responding to the cheers of their followers.

The leisurely progress of the *Huni Moki V* began to worry us, as the captain lingered at each stopping place, bargaining over the price of fish and taking orders for his next unscheduled visit. We suggested that, for an extra five pounds, he might consider speeding things up a little and the response was electric, making us wonder about the profit margins on which he worked. For a day and a night the engine was driven to its limit and we ran at full speed through rainstorms, darkness and narrow channels, feeling guilty when urgent waves from the land were ignored and praying that the tide was right to carry us safely over the reefs. Thankfully we docked at Ambon in time to catch an uncertain connection eastward to New Guinea.

PART FIVE

❧

New Guinea (Irian Jaya)

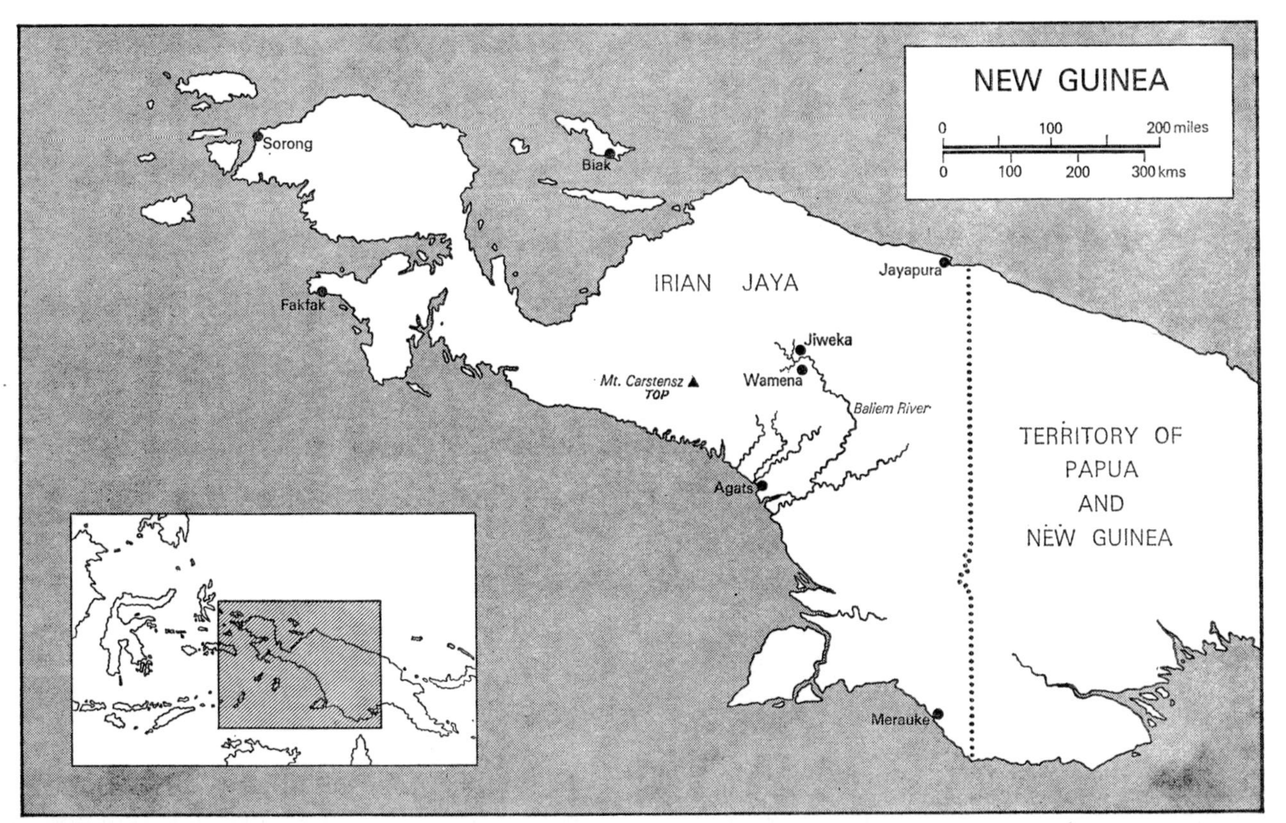
NEW GUINEA
0
100
200 miles
0
100
200
300 kms
Sorong
Biak
Fakfak
IRIAN JAYA
Jayapura
Jiweka
Wamena
Mt. Carstensz TOP
Baliem River
Agats
Merauke
TERRITORY OF PAPUA AND NEW GUINEA

Baliem

❦

NEW GUINEA is the largest island in the world after Greenland. Approximately half the land, and between a quarter and a third of the total population (estimated at three and a half million), now belong to Indonesia. In this area is Carstensz Top mountain, at over five thousand metres (16 500 feet), not only the highest peak on the island, but in the whole of south-east Asia and Australasia. It lies in a region of inaccessible highland valleys stretching for most of the length of the island and inhabited by a rich variety of tribes with many of which contact has only been established in recent years. Around the coasts are extensive areas of lowland rain forest and swamp in the south, often tidal over wide areas, densely overgrown and difficult to penetrate. Much of the rich plant life is still uncatalogued, there are over one hundred species of mammal, almost all marsupial and in some districts the indigenous population remain isolated and continue to practise cannibalism. Where the people came from, and when their migrations took place, is unknown, but in spite of an immediate superficial resemblance to Africans, with their black skins, woolly hair and broad noses, any close relationship has now been disproved, while their affinity with Australian aborigines is only tenuous. The diversity of languages, of which nearly one thousand have been identified, in this the world's most complex linguistic region, as well as of physical and cultural variations, is bewildering but, with the exception of a few pygmy negrito groups, the vast majority of the population are fundamentally similar and classified as Papuans. A further complication, on the Indonesian side, making for confusion over mapping and travel, was that Sukarno changed all the major place names to Indonesian ones. Due to their association with the discredited ex-president, many have been changed yet again so that, for example, Hollandia, the capital, renamed Kota Bahru (new spelling Kota Baru) became Sukarnapura and then Djajapura (new spelling Jayapura), while West New Guinea, later known as West Irian or Irian Barat, has only recently (1973) become Irian Jaya (literally Irian Victory).

The eastern half of the island was divided between the Germans and the British. Bismarck annexed the northern half in 1884 and a British protectorate was declared over the remainder in the same year. Australia took over the German territories at the outbreak of World War I, and administered them subsequently under a mandate from the League of Nations. Since the removal of the Japanese occupying forces involving, incidentally, some of the fiercest fighting in the South Pacific, steps have been taken towards granting full self-government and the creation of a single nation. These were at the time of my visit in the process of completion and the administration was largely in Papuan hands. Full internal self-government was granted to Papua/New Guinea in November 1973.

Shortly after Indonesia achieved its independence President Sukarno laid claim to West New Guinea, believing that the refusal of the Dutch to part with the territory was proof that it possessed immense mineral wealth and, perhaps, also fearing that a continued Dutch presence there represented a threat to his own nation's security. Throughout the 1950s the issue became more explosive until, in 1962, Indonesian forces invaded and a few small battles were fought. The Dutch handed over the administration to the United Nations who, in turn, passed it to the Indonesians in 1963 on the basis that a plebiscite would be held by 1969 to decide the territory's future. However, Sukarno made it clear from the outset that, having once gained possession and renamed the area Irian Barat (West Irian), he did not intend to give it up again. Meanwhile, during the period of '*con-*

frontasi' with Malaysia, Indonesia withdrew from the United Nations. Following Sukarno's fall from power, and the almost complete collapse of the Indonesian economy, the new régime under General Suharto, desperate for international aid, rejoined the United Nations and agreed to honour its undertaking in respect of Irian Barat, but delayed taking any action until the last possible moment. Then, instead of a plebiscite, an 'Act of Free Choice' was arranged and this was limited to one thousand selected Papuan leaders.

The reasons given for this were that it accorded with normal Indonesian practice and that the physical difficulties of carrying out a plebiscite in the remoter parts of the interior made such democratic procedures impossible. Neither of these arguments held much water. The United Nations agreement specifically included, 'The eligibility of all adults, male and female, not foreign nationals, to participate in the act of self-determination to be carried out in accordance with *international* practice.' In Papua/New Guinea the Australians had successfully held general elections in 1964 and 1968 on the one man–one vote system with a population of well over two million and in equally difficult country. But the special representative of the UN Secretary-General to West Irian, the Bolivian lawyer, Fernando Ortiz-Sanz who was sent out to supervise the voting, had no power to tell the Indonesians what they should do and could only protest. The result was a foregone conclusion and West Irian became officially Indonesian.

When the Dutch pulled out of West Irian in 1962 they gave the United Nations thirty million dollars to be used for the development of the territory. On the return of Indonesia to the United Nations fold, the government matched this with an equal amount and a Fund for the United Nations for the development of West Irian (FUNDWI) was established. Initial surveys recommended that priority should be given to agriculture and fisheries, assisting vocational training, education and public health programmes. The emphasis has instead tended to favour the movement of air transport, including training fifty personnel for Merpati, the government-owned airline, with a monopoly of services to West Irian, building roads and setting up a telecommunications network. Some of the FUNDWI staff have expressed disquiet over the concentration on projects which do not directly raise the quality of life for the still primitive overwhelming majority of the eight hundred thousand Irianese. To quote from an article in the *Far Eastern Economic Review* ('Irian's Dilemma' by Barbara Howell, July 1973) to which I am indebted:

> So far the biggest beneficiaries appear to be the Indonesian government, which needs the infrastructure to facilitate its control over the politically discontented Irianese, and the mainly Japanese and American foreign investment companies. Freeport Indonesia, a subsidiary of Freeport Minerals of New York, recently opened a hundred and fifty-three million dollar copper mine in a remote Erstberg mountain area in western Irian Jaya. Almost all of the investment in Irian Jaya is extractive. It is profitable to both the foreign companies and the Indonesian government but adds little to the development of the local people; skilled workers in these companies are mostly foreigners—American, Filipino, Korean, Japanese and Australian.

and

> The Irianese, still resentful of the Indonesian dominance, have little political power or voice in decisions about the use of their resources. They are treated paternalistically by both Indonesians and foreigners.

A certain amount of transmigration of farmers from Java, and settlement by small traders from Celebes (Sulawesi) and the Moluccas, has taken place in recent years. The greater part of the fruit and vegetables consumed in the larger towns, are now supplied by non-Irianese who also control the transport and marketing services. Makassarese and

Butonese have introduced new fishing techniques, particularly lamp nets which produce much higher catches than shore nets, lines and other methods used by the local villages. All this has caused a growing resentment by the indigenous peoples who, even when they can get their products to the markets, find that they are discriminated against, having to sell through middlemen from outside Irian Jaya who have been accused, in a recent survey (*A Survey of the Jayapura Fishing Industry*, Cenderawasih University Institute of Anthropology, Jayapura, December 1972), of creating a monopoly. According to this source the average markup on fish purchased from local fishermen in Jayapura, and sold in the market, was thirty-nine per cent. An attempt was made to develop the trade in vegetables, in particular cabbages, grown by tribesmen in the highlands and flown to the urban coastal centres. But although the aircraft supplying the military and civil installations in the interior regularly return with their holds virtually empty, higher than normal freight and transport rates were charged at all stages of the journey making the operation uneconomic so that it was abandoned.

Describing and commenting on the peoples we saw in Irian Jaya poses me with a major problem. At a time when the remaining colonial territories in the world, be they Portuguese, British, French, or whatever, are under concerted attack in the United Nations and at home; in an era when the suggestion that any one race may have the right to administer another is bankrupt currency; and the very presence of a powerful minority governing a less developed majority inflames liberal passions throughout the world, it is hard to justify the Indonesian occupation of half the island of New Guinea. The dark skinned, frizzy haired Papuans are in no sense kith and kin of the predominately Malay Indonesians; their languages and cultural patterns bear no relation to each other; and their sole historical link is that both formed part of the Dutch East Indies. The original Dutch claim to the western part of the island, arising from the nominal suzerainty of the Sultan of Tidore in the Moluccas, over part of the coast, was about as valid as the Sultan of Makassar's assertion that Australia still forms a part of his overseas territories. Nobody seriously believed that the 'act of free choice', whereby the United Nations handed over the territory to Indonesia, truly represented the informed wishes of the majority of the population, or that a freely conducted plebiscite would have produced the same result.

But the fact remains that the Indonesians are in effective control of the territory and, in spite of some guerilla activity and occasional rebellious and largely uncoordinated demonstrations of dissatisfaction, they show every sign of continuing to be so for the foreseeable future. They are the government and it is they who control the immediate destiny of the tribal and unquestionably undeveloped peoples of the interior, who form the majority of the population. There are those who believe that the Indonesian government should be attacked by all means possible, in an effort to persuade them to abandon the territory. Such counsels may one day prevail and, with the granting of independence to the rest of the island, will certainly gather momentum. The Indonesians themselves, however, have no doubts whatever about the rightness of their presence and, since none of their neighbours is likely to desire or be in a position to make an issue of the question, nothing is likely to change for some time. Meanwhile, the people of the interior are administered and face the day to day problems of survival. Whether a change of régime would improve their lot is at least open to question.

I am, therefore, placed in the position of wishing to discuss the future of these peoples without entering the political arena. For this I shall certainly be criticized by both sides, the Indonesians because I shall question some of their policies and those who oppose their presence for not coming out into the open and attacking the occupying forces. Sitting on the fence is never a comfortable exercise, but since I don't much like the look of the ground on either side I shall try to do so without falling off. One of those who will probably feel that I have let the side down is Mrs Wyn Sargent, an American lady, who caused an international sensation shortly before our arrival when it was learned that she had become the fourth wife of a naked tribal chief in the Baliem valley. At forty-one she was, without doubt, courageous and her condemnation of the ill-treatment of the people with whom she had lived was outspoken and forceful, both before and after her expulsion from Indonesia. We had heard the subject discussed on many occasions during our travels, and I found the reaction of the average Indonesian to the affair interesting. Without exception, they criticized her for what she had done, and many were highly indignant at such interference in their country's affairs by a foreigner. As a byproduct of this irritation, all research by outsiders became suspect and anthropologists were called in to have their papers examined, and permits to undertake scientific work became much harder to obtain. We were, ourselves, warned in Jakarta that we could not have picked a worse time to undertake our own enquiries which contributed to our decision to attempt no more than would be permitted any tourist with rather way out ideas about comfort. But the Indonesians we spoke to seemed not so much to be incensed that she had criticized the government, nor by her comments on the highly touchy subject of Irian Jaya, nor indeed that she had taken the, in their eyes, rather ludicrous step of marrying a 'naked savage'. Rather, the core of their resentment seemed to be that a foreigner should have deliberately insulted them, and denigrated their nation, by choosing a Papuan and an uncivilized one at that. No one believed that she could have done so for love, or even to prove her commitment to helping the tribe. Her action was seen as a piece of gross exploitation, probably for selfish sensationalist purposes, fascinating in its originality, but supremely insulting to a nation proud of its status as the leading South East Asian power. Whatever the truth of the matter it cannot be denied that Wyn Sargent did more in 1973 to draw attention to the existence of Irian Jaya and the fact that all was not well there than any number of learned articles or official reports. However, opinions are divided as to whether on balance she did the cause of the indigenous inhabitants more harm than good, since the sensational aspects of the affair clouded the issues and hardened the authorities' attitude towards criticism.

The flight from Makassar to Jayapura involves an overnight stop on the island of Biak. We were lodged in the airport hotel where our room had a wash basin with the first running water we had seen for several weeks. The only trouble was that the tap was impossible to turn off so that water gurgled noisily down the plug all night. We also met, in the bar, a crowd of expatriate Europeans, Australians and Americans, working for the oil company prospecting offshore who, when they discovered that it was my birthday, jumped at the excuse for a party, invited us back to their mess for dinner and, returning to the hotel bar later, downed every sort of available alcohol indiscriminately and in impressive quantities. Their morale was at a low ebb and they raged against their employers who, perhaps wisely, allowed no drink on the rigs or at the mess, banned wives and forbade fraternization with the locals. They expressed boredom with their jobs and with each other's company, and spent their time counting the days before their next leave. Marika asked if they had struck oil, the one question one doesn't ask an oil man, at which they all became very quiet and evasive, but one of them later opened up to the extent of saying that there is more oil in Indonesia than is generally supposed, and that it is common practice to cap wells as soon as they gush, putting it about that none has been found, while applying for further concessions elsewhere.

Having been kept up until three in the morning we were

not feeling our best at half-past four when woken and told that the flight to Jayapura was about to leave. Life seemed even less bearable when the old DC3, in which we were flying, developed engine trouble almost half way and had to turn around and splutter back. I find modern travel much more soul-destroying when things go wrong than the worst setbacks under primitive conditions. We were told that it was quite normal to be stuck for several days in Biak. Our informant added that the cliffs backing the airfield were riddled with limestone caves where a beleaguered garrison of Japanese soldiers had held out for weeks, in appalling conditions, leaving quantities of grisly remains, and that this was the island's chief tourist attraction, but we were spared the necessity of visiting them by the arrival of a fresh aircraft which we were able to join.

Jayapura is set in a bay of islands and green mountains which has been likened to an eastern Rio de Janeiro. Its architecture, however, fails to live up to the same standard; a few modern concrete buildings line the shore backed by a shanty town climbing the sides of the valley behind. Some of the blame for this must rest with the Dutch, who are reputed, during the three days and nights preceding their final departure, to have thrown an almighty party in the elegant yacht club which graced the harbour. When the last bottle from the cellars had been drunk they burnt the building down. The first thing we noticed was the almost complete absence of Papuans in the street. Indonesians and Chinese manned the shops and offices, and only on the way in from the airport at Sentani did we see gangs of black men working on the road. The waiters in the hotel were Papuan, though not the manager or receptionist, and the few taxis we were able to locate had Indonesian drivers. There are some Irianese in positions of authority and as teachers and policemen, but they seem to have been successfully eliminated from the world of commerce, and real power rests exclusively with the garrison troops under Javanese generals, for much of Irian Jaya is still under military law. With the majority of the Papuan citizens of Jayapura forced to live in the surrounding slums, and deprived of even the limited opportunities for advancement enjoyed under the Dutch, it is scarcely surprising that it is one of the very few cities in Indonesia where the population, fifteen thousand in 1961, is now believed to have actually declined.

Later, I was to pay a brief visit to the eastern part of the island, Papua and New Guinea, as well as the island of Bougainville. The differences were immediately apparent, with an efficient, apparently thriving economy, well run public services and Papuans occupying positions of authority throughout the administration and preparing to take over the running of the country. Even on Bougainville, where the second largest copper mine in the world has had a profound effect on the way of life of the inhabitants, the benefits in terms of prosperity, educational opportunities and self-sufficiency contrasted sharply with the poverty, corruption and sense of hopelessness of Indonesian Irian Jaya. Although the speed of change and the excessive dependence on foreign capital involved will undoubtedly pose problems for Papua/New Guinea during the first years of independence, the Papuans who have been subjected to a century of white colonial rule by the Australians are ironically in a far better position to control their own destinies than those 'liberated' from the Dutch by the Indonesians.

As soon as we had made arrangements to fit in with the Catholic missionary pilot's schedule which would make our later journey to Agats in the south possible, we flew on the daily Merpati flight to Wamena in the central highlands, the only one of Irian Jaya's seven regional centres to lie far from the coast. We took off over the beautiful lake district of Sentani, dotted with attractive islands, where clusters of houses on stilts are reflected in the water. Flying for an hour or more, across a solid carpet of jungle, we crossed low over a range of mountains into the amazing Grand Baliem valley.

The discovery of the valley was one of the last and greatest surprises to be revealed to a world which has mapped and studied the mystery out of most of its remotest corners. In 1938 the explorer, Richard Archbold, landed nearby in a seaplane and looked in briefly before being driven off by the tribesmen. It was forgotten about until 1945 when an American military plane crashed there and the survivors, including a female nurse, were dramatically rescued. Only when the first missionaries, American Protestants, arrived in 1954 was it realized that this high valley, lost and unknown to outsiders from the dawn of time, was densely populated by a sturdy independent people, superb agriculturalists, whose numbers, including related clans from the surrounding hills, have been put as high as sixty thousand. The Dutch government established a post at Wamena in 1956, followed by Catholic priests in 1958. The American anthropologist, Karl Heider, undertook the first scientific studies from 1961 to 1963, returning from 1967 to 1969, and joined for a time by the ill-fated Michael Rockfeller, to participate in making the superb film *Dead Birds* and the beautifully illustrated book *Gardens of War* (published 1970). For much of the time since the Indonesians took over Irian Jaya, outsiders were banned from the territory. Most research is still forbidden and there is not a single anthropologist working in the field today, but tourists can now enter and plans are being made to encourage them. We heard that a huge luxury hotel was to be built at Wamena and saw the draft of a proposed itinerary during which, for an extra seventy-five dollars, 'the tourist gets the opportunity of witnessing the process of killing, slaughtering and primitive roasting of swine, accompanied by breathtaking drum beats and "round the fire" hoopla-dancing'. Or for fifty dollars wild dog hunting on the Baliem river (gun plus ammunition available for rent). However, to date, few tourists have reached the valley, often returning with lurid tales of narrow escapes from the dangerous savages and the rigours of penetrating the primeval jungle. The only accommodation is the *State Hotel*, a long tin shack beside the airfield, or the courteous hospitality of the Catholic missionaries, some of whom have lived there in peace for fourteen years.

The tribes in the valley are usually grouped together under the generic name of Dani. As is so often the case, this is the rather abusive name by which they are known to their neighbours. There are those who say that they should instead be referred to as Baliem people, but since it is simpler and Heider uses the term to describe them, I shall stick to Dani and risk incurring their wrath. My apologies go, in particular, to Father Camps, of whom more later, who I know feels strongly about this. We had seen pictures of the Dani, naked except for their gourd penis sheaths (*kotekas*) with shells or bones through their noses, cowrie shell necklaces and feather headdresses. But with commercial daily flights to Wamena, we had not expected to find them unchanged, surrounding the 'plane as it landed and mingling easily with the few Indonesian soldiers in battle fatigues waiting to go on leave. An Australian, working for the oil company at Biak, had told us how rapidly change had come about in the highlands across the border in Papuan New Guinea. 'Three or four years ago,' he said, 'if you were driving to Mount Hagen and saw a feller in shorts you would stop and ask "What's up? Has someone opened a plantation or has some new missionary arrived?" Now, if you see one bare-arsed or wearing arse-grass he's a real rarity.' We had thought it would be the same in the Baliem valley but, in spite of determined efforts by the government to clothe the Dani, we never saw more than a handful of men in shorts, and only some of the little girls, on their way to the mission schools, wore dresses. Otherwise, the women all wore a narrow net skirt, slung so low beneath their bellies and buttocks that we could never work out how they stayed up. Over their heads they draped a larger net which hung down their backs as a carrier for vegetables, grass, firewood, or whatever other possessions they might have with them. The men seldom carried anything except a spear or fly whisk. Stone axes are rare now, having been largely replaced by metal ones, but most of the digging in the fields is still done (by the women) with stone adzes, the blade a finely shaped and sharpened stone acquired by barter from the distant Yani people, there being no suitably hard rock in the valley.

There is a danger when discussing the needs of such a recently contacted tribe as the Dani of falling into an impossible dichotomy. On the one hand, there is the romantic attitude inspired by a desire to leave them as they are, noble savages at harmony with their environment, while on the other hand the material benefits enjoyed by their developed and independent brethren on, for example, the island of Bougainville appear, on the surface at least, equally attractive. This is a problem common to all discussion of the needs and future of remote tribal peoples and there is no easy or quick answer. Experience throughout the world has shown that rapid change imposed on primitive societies usually causes severe culture shock and emotional disturbance, bringing with it more hardship than benefit. The two examples mentioned here are also, of course, not really valid comparisons as the Bougainvillians have had a long period to adjust to the pressures of contact, the island having been first discovered by the Spanish in 1568 and the first colony established a few years later. The long term intention must be first to help the society concerned to come to terms with the outside world and the dominant society represented by it, and then to develop in such a way as to reap the maximum benefit from the new situation in which its members find themselves. The most vital need, and the most frequent failure, during this period is to get the priorities right. An obsession with superficial changes and conformities, such as wearing European clothes, living in square houses, working regular hours and so on, are of minimal significance compared with understanding the motivations and attitudes of the strangers who have arrived, with their funny ways and fascinating toys. Unless this is understood by those in charge of supervising the change—and it almost never is, whether the process is in the hands of government officials, missionaries or settlers—then the people's confidence in their society and themselves is undermined.

Wamena is not an attractive town, the straight rows of corrugated iron roofs looking out of place in the magnificent setting where blue mountains sweep down to the valley floor, through which the wide Baliem river curves leisurely before plunging into the narrow gorge sealing off the eastern end. We stayed the night there, talking to a young Austrian agriculturalist working on a project for the Catholics. He was full of praise for the Dani as farmers. The soil is rich and they work it skilfully, digging long ditches for irrigation and drainage, and allowing the land to lie fallow between croppings. He felt that the sweet potato, which is the staple diet of the highlands, was a much maligned source of food. 'You have only to look at the Dani to see how they thrive on it and the leaves, which they also eat, contain ten to twelve per cent protein. They grow magnificent cabbages and other vegetables. If they were not prevented from selling these in Jayapura they would have a perfect cash crop, and could buy the things they see in the market but have no money for.' He felt that great danger lay in the removal of the remaining areas of forest, as increasing numbers of military personnel were brought in who used the timber for their houses and barracks. Soon there will be no trees left in the valley. Flying in, I had noticed how few clumps of woodland there were, but instead bare hillsides contrasting with the neat garden plots and round thatched villages. From the air, it had looked more like a rich Alpine valley in Switzerland than the 'primeval jungle' we had been led to expect. No replanting is being done, and promoting this would be an easy way for the government to bring real help to the Dani. Instead, all the emphasis has been on 'operation Koteka', a plan to clothe and civilize the Dani, so paternalistic, ill-conceived and puritanically prejudiced in its priorities as to make one gasp that it could have been drawn up in the twentieth century. But I have a copy of it and, rather than comment, shall simply provide a few quotes so that the reader can see what I mean.

> Socioeconomic conditions among the inland inhabitants are distressing. They live on the products of nature they gather briefly every day, and on the produce of their primitive cultivation, shifting from one place to another.
>
> In outlook, their life is dominated by short range calculation—i.e., to live for one or a few days only.
>
> The inland communities are a relatively easy prey to influence from separatist groups campaigning against the government of the Republic of Indonesia, due to the unsatisfactory social conditions and the pronounced tribalism of the people.
>
> The people remain strongly attached to tribal traditions and customs. This attachment constitutes an impediment in our effort to lead them on the path of development, of social unity and progress in living standards. The chiefs who are, at the same time, warlords, leaders and guardians of tradition and culture, occupy a central position in the tribes.
>
> Their housing is extremely poor. Huts are built of tree poles with thatched roof, primitive structures with no attention given to hygienic or aesthetic factors. The people sleep on the floor, on a bedding of grass, around the fireplace for protection against the cold.
>
> Our objects include teaching the people the importance of having decent living accommodation according to normal village standards, as well as to build houses using locally available materials ... to understand and be willing to

> carry out their duties and responsibilities as family heads and mothers of the household, for children and descendants ... to dress neatly, to cultivate plantations, to care for their animals, to use Indonesian in a limited way, to sing Indonesian songs, to know the names of the Indonesian islands, to cook their food, etc....
>
> Having achieved these objects to form a village and larger community, so as to facilitate the work of officials in guiding and influencing the people toward the attainment of the main objective and, at the same time, to render government administration easier.

Dom Moraes, writing in *The Asia Magazine* (March 1972) about the Baliem valley, sums up Operation Koteka.

> Its aim, in fact, is to change the Dani whether they like it or not, though the Indonesians don't think of it like that. They will deliver trousers to the Dani in much the same mood as that in which Saint Paul delivered the Epistles to the Lacedemonians ... It is bound to be enforced eventually. Money will come into the valley with clothes. The old free life will be finished, and ... [the Dani] ... will become another backward race looked after by a supposedly paternal administration. More children will attend more schools: but what will they learn there which will be of any use to them if they continue to live in the valley? Possibly quite a lot, as the valley changes: but the happiness one feels in the Dani now will have departed, it will have flown beyond the mountains, and nobody will know where they can find that blue bird a second time.

Operation Koteka, apparently the only government plan for the social and economic development of the region, had almost run its two year course, and was scheduled for completion in 1973. Having been an almost total failure it was being replaced by groups of young 'Task Force' volunteers from Java, working on civil projects, building roads, bridges and schools, who were said to be doing a much better job. Experiments with cattle and sheep were being undertaken by the Catholic Mission with some success, although the Dani had not yet mastered the difficulties of guarding the stock which tended to wander into the cultivated crops and eat them in preference to the plentiful grass of the hillsides. Surprisingly, there had been no fish in the valley until the Dutch introduced them in 1960. These were now plentiful in the river and we often saw small boys spearing them in the ditches. Traditionally among the Dani, most of the work in the fields was done by the women, who have the strange custom of cutting off a finger or two each time a husband, child, or loved relation dies, so that many have lost all the fingers from one hand and, sometimes, even some from the other. The men are, therefore, better equipped to undertake such jobs as weaving baskets and nets, plaiting ropes and making necklaces. However, one of their main activities, before the valley was discovered by the outside world, had been battles. More often than not these had been ritual affairs, during which a great deal of energy was expended at the cost of a few injuries, and an occasional death. An important element in any plan affecting the Danis' future must take into account methods of channelling all the pent-up energies of the men in ways which they will find acceptable. Banning fighting and restricting them to the less lethal festivities indulged in at funerals, feasts and other special occasions, have had far-reaching effects on the whole pattern of their lives. Stealing wives and—much more heinous crime—pigs, are now punished by less severe means, while the men are now left with more time on their hands and a propensity to get into trouble. 'Civilizing' the Dani, even assuming that they will be better off at the end of the process than they were before as rich self-sufficient farmers, is never going to be a quick or easy business.

We walked along the valley to the west, finding that on

the well-trodden paths bare feet were greatly to be preferred. I found it a particular relief to shed my shoes as I had broken a toe in Ceram, and unattractive yellow stuff, perhaps with a sliver of bone in it, was beginning to ooze out. Passing fields, in which the rich black earth was being turned before planting, we entered a swampy stretch of forest. Here, the path became wet and muddy so that we sank in to our ankles before reaching hard dry ground again. The numerous Dani we met greeted us cheerfully. Women, carrying loads to the market in Wamena, exchanged the long drawn out cry *'laook'*, sometimes raising a stubby fingerless hand to wave. The men, ambling along with their hands behind their backs and all the time in the world for a chat, had a crisper greeting *'narak'*, usually followed by a firm left handshake and a warm embrace. Since their glistening black bodies were usually daubed with rancid pig fat, as well as being painted on the arms and chest with red ochre, we soon felt, looked and smelt like Dani ourselves. The warmth and genuine affection of these greetings was most endearing. We felt as though our arrival had been expected and looked forward to for months. When we saw that the same joy was manifested when they met each other too, as much between men and women as between members of the same sex, we decided that whatever devils the persistent missionaries were attempting to exorcize from them could not be wholly evil ones.

The suspension footbridge across the Baliem river had recently been washed away in a flood, but repairs were in progress. It swayed alarmingly from side to side as we crossed the wide fast flowing stretch of water and climbed the short slope on the far bank. Here, we came on a wide vista of open uncultivated land. Brown grass, withered by the sun, interspersed with marshes and rocky outcrops; not a soul in sight and only the track, along which we trudged, for another hour or so. The landscape had a wonderful breadth to it, reminding me of the High Atlas in Morocco. The air was fresh and clear in spite of the hot sun, and the only intrusion from the outside world came from an occasional aircraft passing overhead. Over another ridge, and through more cultivated land, our spirits were just beginning to flag in the midday heat when we saw a smart little two storey house with an airstrip beside it, the mission station at Yiwika. Father Camps, who had built the house himself and had lived in Irian Jaya under all its name changes for over twenty years, was at first not sure if he was pleased to see us. Three German ladies had arrived on the mission 'plane that morning, ex-King Leopold of Belgium had been staying shortly before, and he was showing signs of having had enough of tourists. However, after we had shared an excellent lunch with him, and complimented him on his cuisine, he showed us to the most comfortable room in which we had stayed since Jakarta, and said that for the usual modest contribution to mission funds we could stay. He is one of the leading experts on the area, and immediately took a deep interest in the work of Survival International. His approach to the future impressed me by being thoroughly pragmatic which I found a relief after so often having to steer a course between die-hard progressives and hopeless sentimentalists. 'The Baliem people are in danger,' he said. 'Outsiders will come and take their land from them unless they are careful. They don't understand money yet and are easily cheated. Recently, a chief near here sold quite a large field for two spades. His relations were angry and came to me to ask me to sort it out, which I was able to do, but it is becoming harder. At the same time, they are great realists. Seeing the things for sale in the market at Wamena they want them and know that they must change if they are to get them. Education is important.'

'Yes, but what sort of education?' I asked. 'All too often, children in backward areas are led to believe that if they pass their exams the world is at their feet and they will be able to get jobs in the big cities, become President even. Then they are dissatisfied with their own region.'

'I agree, and there is not a lot one can teach these people

about farming here that they don't know already. But they must learn to handle money and look after themselves. Given time they will make excellent traders. I don't know what the future holds for them, but it is too late to stop the clock. We can only try to help.'

On the hill behind the mission, where we had walked to watch the sunset, we made the first of many visits to Dani villages. This one was called Sagatenokoma and lay almost hidden behind some trees, looking from a distance like a diminutive African *kraal.* We passed through the high thatched wooden wall around it by an archway, stepping over a stile which prevented the pigs from wandering in and out. At the far end of an area of bare earth lay the chief's house, the grass thatch of its mushroom-like roof reaching almost to the ground. A man came out of the low door, called *'narak'*, and gestured to us to enter. Inside it seemed pitch dark until our eyes grew accustomed to the gloom, when we were able to see that there was a central fire from which the smoke escaped through the floor of a small sleeping chamber above, pickling the timbers on the way. Two other men were sitting against the circular walls, their feet extended towards the fire. They came forward when we offered around cigarettes, impulsively clasping our hands and, although we could say no more than *'narak'*, making us feel at home. We had a bar of chocolate with us which we shared out to be greeted by appreciative cries of *'wah wah wah'* as they smacked their lips. In return, hot baked sweet potato was scooped out of the fire and the ashes carefully dusted off. They tasted delicious and we did our best to mime enjoyment as effectively as they had. I indicated that I would like to take a photograph and they stared at the camera. When the flash went off they shouted *'Aiee!'* drumming loudly on their *kotekas* with their fingernails and falling about in their enjoyment of the joke.

We were given a guided tour of the premises. Along one side of the central area was a row of similar smaller domed houses in which the wives and small children slept. The women were busy carrying bundles of grass and tending the pigs, which had their own covered enclosure near the entrance. Along the other side was a long low passage, also thatched, in which the women cooked and worked. On a cold night the chief could inspect his whole domain, checking on the pigs, having a bite to eat, and looking in on his wives, without going out of doors. It seemed an excellent arrangement to me and, remembering Operation Koteka, I commented that I was glad to see good use was being made of 'locally available materials' for the building.

Outside, in the garden, they showed us how they were repairing a gap in the fence, slotting the planks between uprights and binding them with plaited ropes. Fruit trees and vegetables were pointed out and we all thanked each other and embraced before taking our leave and climbing a bit further to a vantage point from which we could see the whole valley spread out below. As the sun set, we looked out over a scene of such pristine beauty that we just held hands and watched it drop below the horizon. Smoke drifted up from villages scattered along the valley floor, the river snaked its way past, and across from us, the blue mountains catching the last rays of sunlight ranged away towards Carstensz Top, where the snow never melts.

The ability to produce salt has been the chief source of a commodity for the Dani to barter with their neighbours. Unable to make stone implements themselves, it must have been essential to their economy for centuries. Early in the morning we followed the steep rocky path, through a beautiful forest, to see how it was done. The cool stream splashed down past us, birds sang and bright red and blue flowers sparkled among the rocks. Were I Alfred Russel Wallace, who only touched briefly on the shores of New Guinea, I would have stopped to identify each one; instead, we simply enjoyed their beauty, pausing to rest and cool our feet in the water. The Dani were already on the move, the women loaded with the trunks of banana trees, the men, like us, just going for a stroll to see what was going on. At the top, we found a hive of activity. In a pool, about five metres across and a metre deep, the women stood pounding the stalks to pulp and soaking them in the water. Leaves were also mashed, and every now and then one would break off to straighten her back or chew a piece of especially tough fibre before spitting it back into the water. The men sat in elegant poses on the rocks around a small fire smoking and supervising. The water rises through mineral laden rocks at this point, with a saline content of as much as forty grams per litre. When the banana stems and leaves are thoroughly impregnated they are carried back down to the villages where they are burnt to ashes, which are then used as salt or bartered. The Dani say that they prefer this to imported packet salt and, since the water is probably also rich in other minerals, it could well be better for one.

Throughout the evenings the Dani would wander in and out of Father Camps's house to ask him something, to have a look at his visitors, perhaps bringing a spare *koteka* or stone adze in the hope that they might buy them, or just to sit down and take part in whatever was happening. We bought a fine headdress made of *cus-cus* fur and decorated with parrot feathers and a tall bird of paradise plume. I hesitated for a time as birds of paradise are now rare and rigorously protected in the Australian part of the island, although I noticed in a recent Indonesian guide book that their feathers are still listed as one of Irian Jaya's main exports. But Father Camps said that this one had probably been acquired long before by barter with another tribe, and that buying it was not likely to contribute to the birds' persecution. The Dani were very self-possessed in the European surroundings of the living room with its bookcases, ornaments, tables and chairs. They sat down and picked up a magazine to flick through the pages, or produced mouth harps on which they played absentminded soft notes to themselves. Sometimes, one of the older, dignified chiefs would get up and help himself, with great care, to a cup of coffee from the pot on the sideboard in the corner. There was a young blind boy at the mission whom Father Camps had adopted and given a guitar as he showed signs of being very musical, and would not have had an easy time growing up in his own village. He was the victim of one of the common Dani methods of abortion which, in his case, had failed. The mother, after letting the nails on whatever fingers she possesses grow long, manipulates her stomach until she can feel the foetus's head and then attempts to crush its temples. Occasionally, as in this case, the eyes are caught instead.

During his time there, Father Camps has made a series of short eight millimetre films about various aspects of life in the valley, as well as most of the major festivals and ceremonies. He showed us these, giving a spoken commentary so that, although we were not able to see everything that happens at first hand, we came away with a feeling of having seen a good deal. The Dani crowded in, commenting excitedly when they spotted themselves or their friends on the screen among the crowds of whirling, spear-waving tribesmen celebrating the death of an enemy, or racing round and round, faster and faster, working up for a ritual battle. At the funeral of a great chief the women crouched wailing in rows, their bodies daubed with red, yellow and blue mud, while the men stood, the tears streaming down their faces, around the corpse which sat upright on the pyre before being enveloped in flames and consumed by the fire. 'A Franciscan stays at his mission until his death,' said Father Camps. 'When I go I hope they will cremate me too. It saves so much trouble.'

Occasionally, instead of burning the body, it is smoked and mummified to be preserved as an honoured ancestor. Later, we were to see the famous mummy at Aikima, which was carried out into the open, crouched over in an almost foetal position, but perfect in every detail, the skin shining black like polished ebony and drawn tight over the bones of the face and hands. It is thought to be about fifty years old.

Other films were devoted to agriculture and daily life, including gory scenes of pigs being castrated with sharp bamboo knives, as well as how they are slaughtered by single arrows shot through the heart before they are cooked in a pit on hot stones. There was one excellent educational film made to show the Dani the value of Indonesian rupiah notes of different denominations, with examples of what each might be expected to buy. Also, a hilariously deadpan piece of reportage taken on the occasion when the President's wife had come to Wamena to inaugurate Operation Koteka. Accompanied by stout generals, displaying rows of medals, and elegant Javanese ladies, ill-fitting khaki uniforms were manipulated onto fifty bemused Dani children, who had been kept standing naked in the sun on the airfield for several hours to await having this honour bestowed on them. They were then kept standing for another hour or two while long speeches were delivered to them before the giant Hercules aircraft took off again, with the smug look of a metal *Deus ex Machina*, which has brought instant civilization from heaven.

While we were at Yiwika, Wyn Sargent's husband, Chief Obaharok, called in. He looked fit and well, a burly man with close cropped hair and a narrow headband. Instead of cowrie shells, he wore a stringy necklace and woven bracelets on his wrists and upper arms. With a friendly smile and an easy, relaxed manner, he went and sat in the Father's best wicker chair and accepted a cigarette. Complaining that his bones ached, he said he had come for medicine.

Although he became rather sheepish and embarrassed at the mention of his fourth wife's name, he did not seem in the least abashed by the sensation his marriage had caused and, eyeing the plumpest of the German ladies, suggested that she might like to become number five. His description of the wedding night, translated by the Indonesian school teacher and, I suspect, freely embellished, had the assembled company in fits. Reluctant to consummate the marriage, he said that she had had to prod him up the ladder into the sleeping chamber at the point of a knife, where he had been disappointed to find that she was skinny and 'all covered in plastic'. According to Father Camps, there had been one unfortunate incident, during Mrs Sargent's four months stay, when a Papuan policeman, angered that a white woman should have chosen to live with a Dani rather than a civilized man like himself, had gone to Obaharok's village and fired shots over the Chief's head but that otherwise there had been no local repercussions from the whole affair, and Obaharok had not suffered from it. On my way back to Wamena, I made a short detour off the main path to visit Obaharok's village of Opagima and saw that it had not been burnt down as Wyn Sargent had feared. Photographs of the couple lined the walls of the Chief's house and her house was closed and boarded up awaiting her return.

It seems likely that, following her proposed desire to study the sexual habits of the Dani, and in spite of remarks by her son from a previous marriage widely quoted in the American press as saying that he suspected his mother knew very well what she was doing and would make a lot of money out of it all, Wyn Sargent genuinely wished to help the Dani and bring their plight to the notice of the outside world. It is only unfortunate that she should have gone about this in such a way as to alienate, not only the Indonesians, but also those willing and able to work towards the same end.

Father Camps's awareness of the difficulties of helping the Dani, and his own humility with regard to what he believed he could himself achieve, impressed us deeply. He fully accepted that in physical matters, apart from medical aid, most change was initially likely to be for the worse, since living according to their traditional patterns they are a rich people and excellent farmers. On the other hand, there is certainly room for charity and an infusion of the milk of human kindness into their way of life, but this can only be taught by example and advice. The Dani are not people who can be easily forced to do or not to do anything. Their greatest strength lies in their independence and realism. They are masters at playing rival missionaries and the civil authorities off against each other; given time to absorb all the confusing and far-reaching influences which have descended on them during the last few years, they may well be able to channel their enthusiasm for life in such a way as to succeed and prosper in competition with the modern world. People who have visited the Baliem valley often write about the frightening savagery of the natives, with their flat expressionless yellow eyes, powerful naked bodies and untrustworthy dispositions. They are perhaps alarming at first sight, but the warmth of their interest in strangers, the genuine affection of their greeting, and the peculiar blend of helpfulness, curiosity and pride, convinced me that a child could walk alone in safety from one end of the valley to the other.

The changing Catholic attitude to their mission and their readiness to sacrifice preconceptions in their search for how best to serve the people among whom they work, is well illustrated by a quote from the Bishop of Asmat, summing up one of the wide-ranging conferences they hold from time to time in cooperation with anthropologists and government officials to wrestle with these problems. 'To insist that a people who are labouring under a delusion as to what Christianity is all about, be obliged to follow its tenets, is to negate freedom and respect for man's dignity and integrity—basic rights which we profess to uphold.' Unfortunately, the representatives of the American Fundamentalist churches, also working in the region, take a different view, and are all too often obsessed with the need to save souls at whatever cost to the body. Paradoxically, this attitude is highly reminiscent of the early Catholic Spanish conquerors of South America, with their *autos-da-fé* and fanatical destruction of Aztec and Inca idols. Today the Protestants, often armed—a fact conveniently omitted from subsequent descriptions of their occasional martydom at the hands of irritated pagan savages—force the Dani and other tribes to burn their sacred tribal relics, carvings and ornaments. Total obedience to the tenets of their particular sect, usually based upon the more rigorous demands of the Old Testament, is required, while all who profess to teach alternatives, or even relatively small variations, such as members of the Dutch Reform Church, are branded as incarnations of the Devil whose existence should, if possible, be ignored. Father Camps told me of how, on one occasion, he walked a day's journey to visit a village where a Protestant missionary had recently settled. In the lonely world of an isolated New Guinea highland valley, with the nearest colleague many miles away, one cannot imagine that the sight of another European, dressed conventionally, for Father Camps wore ecclesiastical robes only when performing Mass, would not have been an occasion for extending an enthusiastic welcome and, at least, the offer of a cup of coffee. Instead, the Father sat for an hour on the doorstep of the house while the blond children played in the garden and the missionary studiously avoided acknowledging his presence. When he finally walked away two Dani boys ran after him, bringing a present of some lemons and saying, 'We are ashamed at our Pastor's behaviour and cannot understand it.' The Protestants have refused to participate in any of the conferences, and have only reluctantly agreed that in cases involving life and death the resources of their large fleet of light aircraft might be used. The Catholics have two 'planes servicing their missions, and cooperation would seem only logical in such difficult country, and where spare parts often take months to arrive. The possibilities have often been discussed, but the Protestant pilots say, 'We dare not. If the folks back home got to hear of it they would cut off our funds.' Much of their financial backing comes, ironically, from exclusive white churches in the deep south of the United States, controlling profitable radio and television stations. The arrogance and presumption of such people, with their lack of concern for the long term effects of their actions on the tribes upon whom they force their rigid and outdated beliefs, angers me. But Father Camps's only gentle comment was, 'Things are getting better as younger, more broadminded, men arrive.'

Back in Wamena we did some shopping in the covered market. At one end, half a dozen stalls, run by Chinese merchants, were packed with various foods in tins and packages, reels of cotton, needles, knives, cooking pots, string and soap. Below them, trestle tables were set up in three rows, with a gap dividing the Indonesians, with assorted mirrors, torch batteries, cigarettes, sweets and cutlery, from the Dani, who sat in families, each with a little heap of vegetables or fruit in front of them. These, they had graded according to what they considered were worth a red one hundred rupiah note, and they would accept no others. Pink one thousand rupiah notes had to changed with the Chinese, and when we divided a pile of cucumbers in two and offered fifty rupiahs this was refused. Sensibly, the Dani, having established the value of one unit of the currency which had for them replaced cowrie shells, were not yet ready to negotiate in anything else. Taking as many cucumbers as we could carry easily, we paid one hundred rupiahs to their owner, who had a copious 'pudding basin' hair cut, with coloured feathers framing a smiling face streaked with horizontal red lines and prepared to make off. But the Dani, who was perfectly at ease in the market bustle, wasn't having any of that. We had paid for the whole heap and we were damn well going to take the lot. Our arms were loaded to overflowing and he walked back to the hotel with us, picking up the ones we dropped and then coming into our room to inspect our possessions. None of them appealed to him very much, though he made a halfhearted attempt to give me back the note in exchange for my watch, and with a last affectionate handshake he wandered off hugging himself around the neck against the morning cold.

Asmat

WE flew in the Catholic mission 'plane down the Baliem river, detouring along its length to see if, as I had been told, it really disappeared underground at one point. It doesn't; but it does drop five thousand feet in fifty miles and has never been navigated. I saw no major waterfalls, just almost continuous white water as it passed between high cliffs, curving and twisting down the steep gorge. Inaccessible Dani villages dotted the slopes all the way, and I began to consider the possibility of rafting down the river, stopping wherever possible to climb up and visit them. Heinrich Harrer walked this way in 1961 enduring considerable hardship from the rains and lack of food, and eventually breaking his back in a fall so that the Dani guides carried him out in a litter. But he also described previously uncontacted groups living fully in the Stone Age, and he reached one of the rare quarries where the blue stone for axes is to be found.

Through the mountains we came out onto a flat green vista of swampland, where the densely packed trees, separated only by sluggish muddy rivers, stretched for one hundred and fifty kilometres to the south. An estimated forty thousand Asmatters live on the rivers and in the surrounding jungle, where the single daily tide flows far inland and there is no permanent dry ground. Well over half the tribe have now been contacted and settled in villages on rivers near the coast, but the remaining ten thousand or so still certainly practise cannibalism, for which the whole region was once feared and avoided. Michael Rockfeller, on an expedition in 1962 collecting some of the sensational carvings for which the Asmat people are famous, disappeared when the canoe in which he was travelling along the shore capsized in a storm. His companion stayed with the boat and was later saved, but he attempted to swim to land. He was an olympic class swimmer and, although it is probable that he was drowned, his body was never found and opinions are sharply divided amongst those involved in the subsequent search over the grim alternative. The unlikely hypothesis was put forward in a book (*In Search of Michael Rockfeller*, by Milt Machlin, Putnam's, New York) on the subject that he had been rescued by a party of sea nomads from the Trobriand Islands, who are still keeping him captive there. But another horrifying and grotesquely ironic story still has its adherents, some of whom we met. Shortly before his truly tragic loss, for he was much loved and admired by all who knew him, he had negotiated the purchase of a fine new *bis* pole from a warlike and unpredictable village a short distance up one of the rivers near where he capsized. These poles, up to thirty feet high and exquisitely carved with human figures and phallic symbols, are traditionally made before a village seeks a victim from outside to kill and eat during certain rituals. It is not impossible that members of this particular village, Otsjanep, fishing some way from home, came upon an exhausted man lying in the mangrove swamp and seized the opportunity of avoiding the otherwise necessary armed conflict with their neighbours. Whatever happened, happened a long time ago and the truth will almost certainly never now be known. But the subject is still the cause of much heated argument on the spot.

We arrived at Ewer, the tiny airstrip for Agats, dropping down over the tall trees at one end of the runway and stopping with the aircraft's nose not far from the riverbank. The first Asmatters we saw were a disappointment after the robust muscular Dani. They looked thin in their tattered clothes. Many had pale skins with reddish hair, and several suffered badly from scabies, which seems to arise from a genetic susceptibility rather than malnutrition. The women and girls, with short cropped hair, appeared surprisingly masculine at first sight, and it was hard to distinguish the sexes of the children, except that most of the boys wore shorts, while the girls, if they were not in ragged dresses, had a simple *cachesexe* on a G-string. Agats was a sprawl of nondescript frame houses on piles above the mud, and the 'streets' were elevated and, for the most part, extremely rickety walkways. We received a friendly welcome from the Catholic Fathers, who had built a fine hardwood cloister with guest rooms and a separate building nearby for the nuns who cooked for them. The floors and furniture were made of local mahogany and everything was screened against mosquitoes and spotlessly clean. They belonged to a small order called the Crosiers. Originating in Holland in the twelfth century, they are now based in the United States of America, where they number about two hundred priests and lay brothers. Their main overseas mission is at Agats, but they also work elsewhere in Indonesia as well as in Brazil and a few other places. All we met, with the exception of one elderly Dutch brother, were young energetic Americans with an admirable determination to assess the fundamental needs of the people of Asmat, and let working on their behalf take precedence over indiscriminate proselytization. Bishop Alphons Sowada, who was himself only just forty, invited us to his house and we talked at length about his hopes and fears for the Asmatters. He spoke of his deep concern that if lumber companies move into the region in a big way, as they are showing signs of doing, it will bring little of value to the people since they prefer to import their own labour force. Meanwhile, the sole valuable asset which the Asmatters have, the hardwood trees growing in the jungle, will be removed and they will be left without a basis on which to found an economy. As with the Dani, the desire and need for imported commodities has been created in them and they must be given the opportunity to earn money to acquire them, without becoming dependent upon charity or open to exploitation. The mission has set up a chain of small cooperative saw mills, which the Asmatters operate themselves, and which are slowly beginning to fulfil the need, but they must diversify if they are to prosper, and on the infertile saline swampland where they live alternatives are not easy to find. Sago is their staple diet and grows wild, but already, with an increasing population, concentrated in a smaller area, they are having to go further in search of it. They, themselves, are still not fully aware of the difficulties they face and believe that they can always 'go back to the way things were before' if the going gets too rough. I wondered aloud if they might not be better off in some ways if they did, but had to agree that a taste for civilization is hard to give up once acquired, and anyway where will they go if their forests are cut down and their land taken from them?

The atmosphere at the mission managed to combine a sense of purpose and hard work with a relaxed informality. The ordained priests and the lay brothers, whether committed by their vows to a lifetime with the order, or attached on a temporary basis to help out, were indistinguishable on weekdays in their working clothes. The discipline and self-sacrifice of their lives lay well hidden beneath the surface so that when we all met at mealtimes conversation was animated and cheerful. For example, we talked about the population problem and speculated as to when the Vatican might change its views about birth control. One of the priests told me that under normal circumstances there is not a very rapid population increase in Asmat because sexual abstinence is maintained by taboo from about the fifth month of pregnancy until the resulting child is able to walk. 'It is a common sight here', he said, 'to see a father spending hours encouraging a baby of only a few months to take its first shaky steps!' I even remember the Grace said by one of the least reverential priests, in on a visit from the distant village where he normally lived alone. As far as I can recall it went like this. 'Dear Lord, we thank you for the food we are about to receive and I can only hope it's better than what was dished up last time I was here. Amen.'

The mission maintains contact with its members in the field by means of two heavy old iron boats which chug along barely making progress when current and tide are both against them. Thanks to the Bishop's generosity, we were able to hitch lifts on these as they carried supplies up to some of their out stations. Unless going up the Agats river itself these journeys always had to be begun by a detour out to sea and along the coast before entering the river on which the particular village to be visited lay. The Brothers enjoyed speculating on the ideal sort of boat for their purposes, and how much easier life would be with faster lighter craft. But the sea can be very rough and storms blow up suddenly, ruling out anything too small, while Agats is so cut off from the outside world, with only a very occasional visit from a large ship and all normal supplies brought in by air, that they felt that a commitment to less reliable outboard motors would be risky. And so, surrounded by diesel fumes, we slipped slowly past the endless mudbanks and the overhanging dank greenery. Occasionally we passed side streams, and could for a moment look into the hidden world behind which wild pig and crocodiles, hornbills, kingfishers and snakes conduct their own private battles. Wild pig are plentiful, but Indonesian traders using high-powered rifles are increasingly hunting the crocodiles to extinction. One seven metres long giant, which had so far escaped and had eaten several unwary swimmers, was spotted within a couple of kilometres of Agats while we were there, sunning himself on the bank. Some of the creeks had fish traps made of stakes fencing off their mouths to catch whatever came in on the tide, and now and then we glimpsed a temporary camp with houses built like wigwams out of poles and branches. The Asmatters propel their narrow dugout canoes standing up wielding long paddles in unison with superb balance. The sight of eight men moving as one, their canoe gliding across the surface at a speed which would have brought them no discredit at Henley Regatta, while their reflections raced them in the still waters, is unforgettable. One crew hailed us as we passed, and we stopped thinking to buy some fish. Instead, they showed us a huge wild pig they had just killed, and agreed with our boatmen to exchange the four haunches for sticks of tobacco. Still standing up, they chopped them off and passed them up without rocking the canoe at all, and accepted the tobacco with beaming grins. Since I had just bought it at one hundred rupiahs (ten pence) per stick to give away as presents, and since each leg must have weighed at least ten pounds, it was not difficult to calculate that we were paying less than one penny per pound for prime fresh pork, which we felt must be some sort of world record. Deeply impressed, Marika promised to send the mission a recipe for preparing salami.

Longhouses in which the Asmat used to live were abolished by the Dutch in accordance with the familiar desire to settle the people in 'modern' accommodation, in 1954, and we were depressed by the regular rows of shacks, all built to the same pattern, which now comprise most of their villages. Unlike the Dani, the Asmatters have quite a long history of intermittent contact, including a considerable amount of activity in their area during the Second World War, and some previous trading on the coast. However, for the most part, their territory was avoided and outsiders were, with good reason, afraid to penetrate the rivers. Now, the majority of those contacted wear clothes which they keep on until they literally rot off their bodies. They also seem to be suffering from a good many more diseases and general ill health than the Dani. A recent epidemic of whooping cough had killed a large number—twenty in Erma alone, the first village we visited. There may be all sorts of reasons for this contrast and I have no other evidence to go on but hindsight. Still, one possible conclusion that might be drawn, although it will doubtless irritate many even to suggest such a thing, is that the Asmatters, who took to clothes fairly quickly but perhaps without accepting the necessary régime of washing both themselves and their garments regularly, have suffered a decline in health and a susceptibility to new diseases; while the Dani, by and large rejecting clothes and continuing to cover themselves with pig fat and remain unwashed, have tended to stay in better health. There could be a moral to draw in this. If clothes are worn for reasons of prudery rather than for comfort and convenience, there may be a greater danger of their being misused.

The few last days of our journey, now that we had reached the eastern corner of Indonesia, passed pleasantly as we lay on deck in the sun, cruising around the rivers of Asmat and calling in at villages, blurred now in memory to a single pattern. Father Dale and Father Dave, Brothers Clarence and Jim took us round, guided us along the catwalks, showed us beautifully carved canoes and introduced us to the men who could still make the characteristic statues and *bis* poles. Hospitably received, enveloped in kindness and entertained with stimulating conversation, we could not understand why we had so little energy. We were more tired than we realized after three months of constant pressure, travel, change, slight danger, great excitement, but never a moment to really relax. Marika, after staying in excellent health and never flagging for an instant, was heading for a crisis during which she later lost two stone. As she is normally about eight stone this meant that she practically vanished into thin air. Physicians of the utmost fame in London, assuming that she must have picked up some rare eastern bug, conducted every conceivable test. Their conclusion was that it was nothing more than starvation brought about by burning up more energy than was being replaced, and that this had started her on a downhill spiral which they only just checked in time. I simply felt very very tired. The knowledge that nothing but bottomless, waterlogged mud lay all around us and below us gave me a feeling close to vertigo, and I longed for rocks, slopes and the cool fresh breeze of the mountain top.

At Ayam, the largest village in Asmat, we finally met Father Frank Trenkenshuh with whom I had corresponded, imagining him to be an elderly erudite greybeard. Trenk, as he is known to all, is a qualified anthropologist and, with the bishop, one of the Crosiers most intimately concerned and involved in the whole knotty question of the Asmatters' future. Tall, good-looking and two years younger than me, he is a man of boundless enthusiasm and good humour. For him, problems are sent to be solved, and while he is probably more aware than most of the dangers ahead he inspires confidence that they can and will be tackled. 'If both the culture and natural resources of Asmat are removed, what will happen?' I asked. In the first place he is working hard to regenerate the tremendous artistic talent of the tribe. A museum is being opened at Agats, not just as a record of the past and a showplace for tourists off the cruise ships which will soon start arriving, but also an inspiration to the Asmatters themselves to take a pride in their rich heritage. Then, the timber cooperatives are expanding so that at least a part of the area's potential benefits the indigenous inhabitants directly.

'The people must learn to stand on their own feet,' Trenk went on. 'They must learn to find their own way of coming to terms with new situations. Charity is no use. For example, I always burn or bury all my trash. Even though much of what I throw away would be used by them, I won't have them grubbing through it and one day remembering that they had to do this. I don't even give them used tins. If they bring me something small I might give a tin as a present. Normal payment here is with tobacco. I insist on making most of mine cash so that they have some and learn how to use it. They are so often exploited by traders over money. It is urgent that they are taught to avoid this. Often a man will go into a shop with, say, a one thousand rupiah note. After he has bought a little tobacco, some nylon line and a few fish hooks, he will be given a heap of five and twenty-five rupiah notes as change. He comes away with his shopping and more notes than he went in with, thinking he must have done well out of the deal.

'As to the future, I really don't know what the next fifteen or twenty years will bring. The population is growing, their way of life is changing and their needs expanding. But it is outsiders who are deriving most of the benefit from the shops and the lumber business. Only the mission has kept the people going so far, and this is a real danger. They should not be dependent on us. So many changes of attitude have been forced on them by successive administrations. At first they were told to burn down their longhouses and destroy their carvings. Now, they are told to start making artifacts again so as to encourage tourism. Social centres are being built, but most of the old longhouse activities are prohibited due to their association with headhunting and the old days. It's like making people build a church and then not allowing them to worship in it.'

Consideration of the Asmatters' future in these terms seemed to me to approach the root of the problem and the philosophical implications of such thinking, touching upon the very nature of man, takes us a step nearer to finding valid hypotheses on which to work. If one accepts that, allowing for certain relatively insignificant variations, all members of the human race are equal and capable of fulfilling a potential far greater than that which each of us usually does achieve, then the stimulus to create must to a great extent depend upon the cultural environment in which we grow up and live. Man's capacity to break out of his culture and conquer new worlds, whether physical or intellectual, is what truly makes him different from animals, but he must equally have a rich, strong culture out of which to break.

The missionary who cannot face his own religion as a complete idea within himself but needs to assert and justify it by bringing it to others and making them conform to his model, is running away from himself. Just as a wise man can achieve serenity through concentrating his own mind, so the isolated tribe may achieve a higher satisfaction within its own culture. Outside influences will certainly impinge but we do not have the right to impose fundamental changes of attitude. The missionary who dedicates his life to helping others, without preconceptions and implied condemnation of beliefs and modes of life which differ from his own, is fulfilling a valuable and admirable function. If he has also taken vows of celibacy and poverty, he is relieved of the responsibilities of family and career which make it even harder to endure the loneliness and sacrifice of total commitment. Such men, however, are rare.

Tobacco was unknown in Asmat, at least on the coast, prior to contact. It was the first need for something they did not already have which was created in them, and now they are almost desperate for it. It is too late to reverse the trend as other needs grow, and the only hope is to seek a sound economic basis providing a cash surplus so that the Asmatters can achieve independence from both charity and exploitation. It is desirable that they should diversify away from timber, and there is room for much research in this area. Sago has, at the moment, no great value as a crop for sale for processing, but it is such a rich food source, and grows so freely in tropical swamps where other forms of agriculture are hard to develop, that I feel sure it has untapped potential. Forms of animal husbandry also open up interesting possibilities. The mission did introduce a small herd of Javanese cows a few years ago, which failed to thrive due to the wetness and mineral deficiencies in the vegetation, but no one has yet tried water buffalo which might find the conditions more favourable. Experiments could also be made with chickens, ducks, goats and fish ponds, opening up extensive possibilities for research by a tropical agriculturist. Other fields, which Trenk believes could be profitably studied, include pottery using suitable local clay from the rivers and the Asmatters' potent talent as artists to create a new industry, as well as the whole question of education and its proper adaptations to the people's particular needs. On the rivers we had seen quantities of crown pigeons, large rather stupid birds, which make excellent eating and, carried away in the search for ideas, I had a vision of vast domesticated flocks trained to feed in the jungle, returning to their dovecotes when fat and succulent, to be plucked and exported to Europe and America as a new delicacy.

There is, however, no doubt that the Asmatters face a long uphill struggle if they are to avoid becoming a depressed social problem like their neighbours in the region of Mimeka, who have been in contact far longer and have degenerated to become one of the most hopeless and discontented peoples in Indonesia. Thanks to the presence of the Crosiers, they stand a good chance of making it—whatever 'it' is. But then, trying to answer that question for tribal peoples is, I believe, what Survival's work is all about. In three months we had only seen a small part of the problem in Indonesia, and we had only scratched the surface of possible answers; but that large numbers of tribes, in need of help and support if they are going to survive, exist we were no longer in any doubt.

Conclusions

THE problems affecting tribal minorities in Indonesia do bear many similarities to those which beset the Indians of South America. The major difference is that throughout most of this vast country, with the fifth biggest population in the world, there is, with the exception of the Papuans of New Guinea, one race of many peoples. They think of themselves as one people and are superstitious regarding each other's beliefs and traditions, which they respect and consider valid. Here, change is happening so fast, and attitudes towards development are being formed at such a rate that the main danger lies in the problems of tribal minorities being overlooked, rather than in their being insoluble. While protection and preservation are undoubtedly needed in some cases, there is hope that in the long run respect for alternative cultures may find its place in the national ideal alongside the current obsession with trying to copy the Western materialist dream. I believe that, prompted by the growing energy and resource crisis, the world is beginning to recognize this fact and that we may become more tolerant of the differences between us. If those differences stem from separate cultures developed over thousands of years, then we should go further and, not only tolerate them, but also respect them. Indonesia is in a unique position to work in this direction and avoid the mistakes of so many other developing nations.

Peoples which are called primitive, simple, backward, unacculturated, savage, tribal, native, isolated or whatever, are not essentially different from us. The evolutionary separation from other men is as nothing when set against the aeons of time during which we were all hunters, the few thousand years since the earliest beginnings of agriculture and the domestication of animals, let alone the mere flicker of history since industrialization commenced. But they seem strange—and, to some, inferior—because they express themselves differently; their vision of the world is not the same as ours and, while possessing a rich and harmonious concept of life, they lack the narrow blinkers of a scientific, materialist ideology which assumes the ability to control and understand all things but has in truth barely scratched the surface of life's diversity. Their main hope lies in the impending sense of change which is sweeping through the world of ideas. Man's confidence in the power of his recently acquired wisdom is shaken by his sudden realization that the resources of the planet are finite and a growing awareness that both man and the universe he inhabits are more complex than was until recently believed. If this attitude continues to develop to the stage where the arrogance of the last century or so is replaced by an inquiring humility in the face of the problems which beset us, then our attitude towards those remaining societies, which have not yet accepted the dubious tenets of our own, may change. Then, instead of having to search in the dark for new philosophies there will still be working models to learn from; not to copy slavishly, for it is no less impractical to suggest that we can survive without technology as it is to believe that universal happiness can be achieved through uncontrolled growth, but by combining the knowledge and approach of both.

Our society's fragility and its dependence on resources and interrelationships beyond our control has been thrown into sharp relief by the recent oil crisis and the chain reaction of international financial upheavals, industrial unrest and shortages of materials which it sparked off. Meanwhile, throughout the world nations' efforts to exploit the remaining untapped areas of forest, wilderness and swamp have been intensified in the race to grab as much of the global cake as possible, without thought for the effect this will have upon their neighbours and upon the vital basic food chains upon which we all depend. Removing the vegetation in tropical rain forests can alter the climate and cause erosion which in turn silts up the rivers' estuaries and the alluvial plains of the coast. Drainage schemes in marshland areas combined with industrial pollution and a general neglect of ecological imperatives in search of short-term economic gains can have far-reaching effects on maritime and estuarine birds and fishes which are critically interdependent. The remaining so-called marginal areas of the world make an essential contribution to maintaining the health of the whole planet and where man has learnt to live in close harmony with these areas his rôle should not be overlooked.

Much further study is needed. Too little is known about the peoples and cultures of the archipelago, their needs and their vulnerability. We should find out why the Hua Ulu are not breeding; we should conduct medical research among the other tribes and find out which new diseases, introduced from outside, represent a threat to them. Their needs and what changes, if any, will benefit them should be studied. The people should be given a chance to express their own opinions about whether they want to 'stay in their own culture' or adopt new ways; whether they want to retain their tribal lands and way of life, or move to a new urban environment where, although they may be easier to administer, they will become an even greater social problem. On the whole, from what we saw, most would to a greater or lesser extent wish to resist change, although in, for example, the case of the Bataks there is no great desire to retain the physical manifestations of their culture, and the same will soon be true of the Toraja. However, it will be a long time before these sorts of considerations will apply to people like the Mentawai or the Hua Ulu.

There is an element of *Catch 22* about the whole Indonesian enigma. The country, if one thinks of it as a country and not just a collection of diverse cultures and separate island people, is rich in ancient traditions and varied ways of life. At the same time, those in authority are all too often blind, greedy, corrupt, inefficient and helpless at coping with all the exploding problems they now have to face. If every effort is made to copy the western world and adopt its patterns of life, this will tend to foster the worst elements in the country. If, on the other hand, the cultures are isolated and not given the chance to play their part in the country's future, then the technologically superior western oriented elements in the country simply have a free hand to direct affairs in their own way. The whole situation is far too complicated for me to presume to suggest easy remedies. But I did come to learn that most Indonesians have very little knowledge about their own countrymen, about their nation's real potential and the dangers ahead. There is a vast ignorance about the other inhabitants of the archipelago, not only the one-sided view of the majority of the population living in Java, but also the ignorance of peoples in the outer islands, living close to one another, but suffering from the dislikes and suspicions of next-door neighbours. At the same time, paradoxically, this is combined with a great fear of other peoples' powers and mystical abilities. I remember an ex-Governor of Ambon telling us that he firmly believed that one of the tribes on Ceram had the ability to fly through the air and bring you harm if you angered them.

Against all this is set the evident urgent desire for all the worst aspects of western plasticry, and a rejection of their own skills and techniques. It is hard to see where this can lead except to a general degrading of standards and an arrival at the lowest common denominator of poverty in all respects. Perhaps the most useful thing an outsider can do is simply to suggest that the Indonesians should look more within their own country for ways of coming to terms with the future, and place less reliance on attempting to copy our society. In spite of the tremendous population problem, Indonesia is rich and few people starve. We are just beginning to learn how dependent we are on resources from outside to maintain our economy and standard of living. Indonesia offers a golden opportunity for a nation to choose to develop along different lines, favouring low impact technology and a more stable basis for feeding and satisfying the needs of its peoples.

Ceasing to try and change 'different' minorities without a full idea of the alternative being offered would be one way of coming to terms with this problem. The wastage of human talent, originality and knowledge at a time of growing conformity, accompanied by new crises of human life and how to support it, is something which we cannot afford to allow to take place. If we are not prepared to stand idly by and confess that we do not know the answers, then we should first seek the people themselves and try, at least, to assess the problem. This is as far as I am able to see into the future.

What surprised me most about the time we spent in Indonesia, and the people we met who lived there and had considered the country's future, was how many had already come to the conclusion at which I had only guessed, that this country holds in its hands many of the keys to a stable and successful future. These thoughts did not arise out of a nostalgic wish to see the clock put back to the days of the great Rajahs, and to a time when colourful pageantry took place and beautiful things were made, when tribal cultures were strong and flourishing and cannibalism, headhunting and human sacrifices were common. No one is foolish enough to pretend that those days were any happier, or that there was any less cruelty and hunger. The feeling I so often encountered came rather from a fear that a blind worship of progress was destroying too much that was of value, not just aesthetically but also in practical terms, so that there was a grave danger that it might soon be too late to avert a major catastrophe. Ways of life which had evolved over hundreds, even thousands, of years were being changed overnight without careful consideration of the consequences, so that there was a strong possibility that the remaining untapped jungles and fertile seas of a great nation would be laid waste. For instance, a barium sulphate factory was planned for Makassar. Without the strictest pollution control, which was not planned in this case, such factories are among the most lethal of man's inventions, the cooling water killing all marine life and the smoke bearing deadly fumes wherever the wind blows. No other country in the far east would allow such a factory to be built anywhere near them, and even the American engineers, sent out to approve the site, said that a worse one could hardly have been found, lying next to a bakery and beside a harbour from which a fishing fleet of small boats set out daily. But the Indonesian government were said to be delighted at this manifestation of progress, and the revenue which it would bring in, giving the go ahead for work to commence.

Deforestation and all its attendant dangers, I have spoken of, but I also met no one who viewed with equanimity the sweeping plans proposed for agricultural intensification. Of course, the Indonesians must grow more food if they are to feed their exploding population, but the way to do this is by encouraging those who know the land best to produce more, increasing the financial incentive to do so, and conducting research into how these methods might be improved; not by taking the land from them and introducing heavy machinery, and costly capital equipment, which has been shown in so many parts of the world to produce, in the long run, a much lower output per acre at much higher cost. Centralized governments are always prone to such follies, and few are more centralized than Indonesia's; yet the key which that country holds in its palm, if it would but pause for a moment in its insane rush to emulate the western world, is that it possesses the richest fund of cultural diversity of any nation; a priceless source of pride and energy which, given the right stimuli, could generate the necessary will to tackle all these problems and produce sound solutions, tempered to the various peoples' own abilities and aspirations. No single course of action will make Indonesia's future easy. The country, like every other, faces accelerating difficulties of growing complexity. But this fundamental factor in the equation seems to be entirely lacking from official thinking, which is no less than tragic when so much of the cultural vitality, lost elsewhere in the world, exists throughout the islands. This is why I believe it is important not to force change on all who differ from the official norm, and why a reason exists for fostering the survival of the hundred and fifty or so Hua Ulu, no less than the one and a half million Bataks; not their survival simply as anonymous members of a disorientated homogeneous society, but as Hua Ulu or Batak, loyal to a greater national identity, but also secure of their place in their own environment.

The national motto of the Republic of Indonesia is *Bhinneka Tunggal Ika*—Unity in Diversity. The nation is certainly diverse and, in spite of nearly thirty years of conflict and economic crisis since independence, has remained united. One of the lowest per capita incomes in the world and a growing population largely dependent on agriculture contrast with relatively abundant resources now being extracted by foreign companies and some of the most fertile soils in the world. Scattered over three quarters of a million square miles of islands live more than three hundred ethnic groups administered from the small overcrowded island of Java. Economically and politically the country faces a long, hard road if it is to achieve stability and prosperity.

There are great opportunities, but there are also immense dangers ahead. Seeking short-term gains from the unexploited outer islands poses severe ecological risks. Attempting to make the numerous cultures conform to a standard pattern will create divisive stresses. If an acceptance of diversity is seen as the central theme of the nation, essential to its unity, then this should apply at all levels. By respecting its economically and socially least powerful members, the government would not only demonstrate its adherence to the spirit of its national slogan but might also in doing so discover sound principles upon which to build for the future.

CONCLUSIONS

My object in writing this book has been firstly to show that in the time we spent in Indonesia we saw enough to know that there are cultural and tribal minorities facing very real problems as progress in all its forms sweeps over them; and secondly to attempt to demonstrate that there is justifiable cause for concern over their fate. Such concern is now accepted as valid in the case of the Indians of South America, although little enough is done about it. How much more reason there should be for us to be worried about the future of those far greater numbers of minorities in Indonesia, who do not yet, and may never be able, to identify with the national desire to enter the modern world. Setting aside my own private suspicion that their way embodies as much viable long-term hope for the future as ours, and fully accepting that we live in a world beset by change, my plea is simply that they should be given time and help to draw their own conclusions.

Bibliography

Robert Allen, *Natural Man* (Aldus Books, 1973)

John F. Cady, *Southeast Asia. Its Historical Development* (McGraw-Hill, 1964)

Robert Gardener and Karl Heider, *Gardens of War* (Random House, 1968; Andre Deutsch, 1970)

Adrian A. Gerbrands, *Wow Ipits* (Mouton & Co., 1967)

Karl Heider, *The Dugum Dani* (Viking Fund Publications in Anthropology No. 49, 1970)

Jones, Howard Palfrey, *Indonesia—The Possible Dream* (Harcourt, Brace, 1971)

Edwin Loeb, *Sumatra—Its History and People* (Oxford University Press, 1935; reprinted 1972)

Milt. Machlan, *The Search for Michael Rockefeller* (Putnam, 1972)

Peter Matthiessen, *Under the Mountain Wall* (Heinemann, 1963)

G. J. Missen, *Viewpoint on Indonesia* (Nelson, Australia, 1972)

James L. Peacock, *Indonesia: an anthropological perspective* (Goodyear Publishing, 1973)

Peter Polomka, *Indonesia Since Sukarno* (Penguin, 1971)

Robert Pringle, *Rajahs and Rebels. The Iban Under Brook Rule 1839-1939* (Macmillan, 1970)

Michael Rockefeller, *The Asmat* (Museum of Primitive Art, 1967)

John Ryan, *The Hot Land. Focus on New Guinea* (Macmillan, 1970; paperback edition, Macmillan, Australia, 1971)

Fritz A. Wagner, *Indonesia* (McGraw-Hill, 1959; Methuen, 1959)

Alfred Russel Wallace, *The Malay Archipelago* (First published Macmillan, 1869. Republished in 1962 by Dover Publications; Constable, 1969)

Harry Wilcox, *White Stranger. Six Moons in Celebes* (Collins, 1949)

Richard Woldendorp and A. H. & Y. Johns, *Indonesia* (Nelson)

Bulletin of Indonesian Economic Studies (Department of Economics, Research School of Pacific Studies, Australian National University, 1972 & 1973)

Irian. Bulletin of West Irian Development (Institute for Anthropology, University of Cenderawasih, 1973)

Index

INDEX

THAILAND
KHMER REP.
SOUTH VIETNAM
M A L A Y S I A
BRUNEI
SABAH
MALAYA
SARAWAK
BORNEO
SUMATRA
Djakarta
JAVA
I N D O N
INDIAN OCEAN
0
1000 miles
0
1000 kms